THE 100+ SERIES™

READING COMPREHENSION

Essential Practice for Advanced Reading Comprehension Topics

Grade 2

Carson-Dellosa Publishing LLC

Greensboro, North Carolina

Credits

Content Editor: Angela Triplett
Proofreader: Carrie Fox

Visit *carsondellosa.com* for correlations to Common Core, state, national, and Canadian provincial standards.

Carson-Dellosa Publishing LLC
PO Box 35665
Greensboro, NC 27425 USA
carsondellosa.com

© 2015, Carson-Dellosa Publishing LLC. The purchase of this material entitles the buyer to reproduce worksheets and activities for classroom use only—not for commercial resale. Reproduction of these materials for an entire school or district is prohibited. No part of this book may be reproduced (except as noted above), stored in a retrieval system, or transmitted in any form or by any means (mechanically, electronically, recording, etc.) without the prior written consent of Carson-Dellosa Publishing LLC.

Printed in the USA • All rights reserved.

ISBN 978-1-4838-1560-2
04-189197784

Table of Contents

Introduction

Organized by specific reading skills, this book is designed to enhance students' reading comprehension. The engaging topics provide meaningful and focused practice. The reading passages are presented in a variety of genres, including fiction, nonfiction, and poetry. Subject matter from across the curriculum, including topics from science, history, and literary classics, deepens student knowledge while strengthening reading skills.

The grade-appropriate selections in this series are an asset to any reading program. Various reading skills and concepts are reinforced throughout the book through activities that align to the Common Core State Standards in English language arts. To view these standards, please see the Common Core Alignment Chart on page 4.

Common Core Alignment Chart

Common Core State Standards*		Practice Page(s)
Reading Standards for Literature		
Key Ideas and Details	2.RL.1–2.RL.3	6, 10, 11, 12, 19, 27, 36, 48–51, 55, 57–65, 67, 70, 72, 75, 80, 82–89, 94–97, 101–105, 111, 112, 114, 115, 117, 122
Craft and Structure	2.RL.4–2.RL.6	6, 8–11, 104–109, 111
Integration of Knowledge and Ideas	2.RL.7–2.RL.9	16, 17, 19, 27, 30, 31, 48–51, 57, 60, 61, 64, 67– 69, 82, 83, 88, 89, 92, 93, 98, 99, 103, 122
Range of Reading and Level of Text Complexity	2.RL.10	6, 8–12, 16, 17, 19, 27, 30, 31, 36, 48–51, 57–65, 67–70, 75, 76, 80, 82–89, 92–99, 101–109, 111, 112, 114, 115, 117, 122
Reading Standards for Informational Text		
Key Ideas and Details	2.RI.1–2.RI.3	5, 7, 13–15, 18, 20–26, 28, 29, 32–35, 37–45, 47, 52–54, 56, 66, 71, 73, 74, 77–79, 81, 90, 91, 100, 110, 113, 116, 118–121
Craft and Structure	2.RI.4–2.RI.6	5, 12–15, 18, 20–22, 24, 26, 35, 37–46, 53, 54, 56, 66, 71, 73, 74, 77–79, 81, 90, 91, 100, 110
Integration of Knowledge and Ideas	2.RI.7–2.RI.9	28, 32, 33, 39, 44–47, 52, 53, 71, 81
Range of Reading and Level of Text Complexity	2.RI.10	5, 7, 13–15, 18, 20–26, 28, 29, 32–35, 37–47, 52–54, 56, 66, 71, 73, 74, 77–79, 81, 90, 91, 100, 110, 113, 116, 118–121
Reading Standards: Foundational Skills		
Phonics and Word Recognition	2.RF.3	41, 42, 93
Fluency	2.RF.4	113
Writing Standards		
Text Types and Purposes	2.W.1–2.W.3	72, 76, 77, 92, 93, 106, 107
Language Standards		
Vocabulary Acquisition and Use	2.L.4–2.L.6	21, 38, 56, 78, 79, 100, 101, 110

* © Copyright 2010. National Governors Association Center for Best Practices and Council of Chief State School Officers. All rights reserved.

© Carson-Dellosa • CD-104840

Name_____

Read the story.

A Falling Star

Have you ever seen a falling star? Falling stars are not really stars. They are small pieces of rock. The rocks fall through the sky. They get hot and burn. The rocks look big because they give off light. That is why they are so bright. Another name for a falling star is a **meteor**.

1. Write **1**, **2**, and **3** to put the steps in order.

_____ The rocks look big because they give off light.

_____ The rocks fall through the sky.

_____ The rocks get hot and burn.

3. Why do falling stars look so bright?

A. because they are falling

B. because they give off light

C. because they are rocks

D. because they are stars

2. What is another name for a falling star?

A. burning rock

B. falling rock

C. meteor

D. night sky

Read the story.

Jan's Job

Jan loved her job. Jan juggled. First, Jan juggled jars of jam. Second, Jan juggled jars of juice. Next, Jan juggled jars of jelly beans.

Then, Jan juggled Jay the jackrabbit. But, Jay the jackrabbit jerked and jumped away with the jam and the juice and the jars of jelly beans.

1. Look at the pictures. Use **1**, **2**, **3**, and **4** to number the pictures in the order they happened in the story.

_____   _____   _____   _____

2. What do you think Jan will do now?

_____

_____

_____

© Carson-Dellosa • CD-104840

Read the story.

Fishing for Light

What kind of fish comes out only at night? The flashlight fish! It has a special way to stay safe. It has lights under its eyes.

What does it do to stay safe? First, it uncovers its lights. It can do this like you can open your eyes. Next, the flashlight fish swims in a straight line. A dangerous fish follows the lights. Then, the flashlight fish covers its lights. Last, it turns and races away. The dangerous fish cannot see where the flashlight fish has gone. The flashlight fish is safe.

1. Read the sentences. Number them in the correct order.

    _____ The flashlight fish covers its lights.

    _____ The flashlight fish turns and races away.

    _____ The flashlight fish swims in a straight line.

    _____ The flashlight fish uncovers its lights.

2. Where are the lights on the flashlight fish? _____

3. When does the flashlight fish come out? _____

© Carson-Dellosa • CD-104840

Read the story.

Clowning Around

Zane blows out his candles. A clown tumbles in through the door. She blows up balloons. She twists them and turns them to make dog shapes. Then, she stands on her head and plays a song on the harmonica. Smoke appears, and the clown disappears. This is Zane's best birthday party ever!

Cut out the pictures on page 9. Glue them in the correct order.

1.

2.

3.

4.

5.

© Carson-Dellosa • CD-104840

Read the story.

Ring Around the Moon

Sally Space Officer flew on her nightly patrol. "How are you, Pluto?" she asked.

"Fine," answered Pluto.

"Having a good night?" she asked Venus.

"The best." Venus glowed.

When Sally flew close to Mars, she worried. Mars frowned. Tears rolled down Mar's craters and made huge pools. "What is the matter, Mars?" she asked. "How can I help?"

"One of my moons got a ring for a gift. But the ring is lost. My moon is so sad. Now it does not give any moonlight. My poor moon!" Mars sniffled.

"I have an idea!" cried Sally Space Officer. She raced off toward Saturn. She flew back carrying a sparkling ring. "Will this help?" she asked.

Mars smiled a smile that crossed all Mar's craters. Sally tossed the ring to Mar's moon. Instantly, the moon grew bright.

"All is well with my planets," said Sally.

© Carson-Dellosa • CD-104840

Name_____

Answer the questions.

1. Who is Sally checking on during her nightly patrol? _____

2. Why is Mars sad? _____

3. Cut out the pictures. Glue them in the correct order.

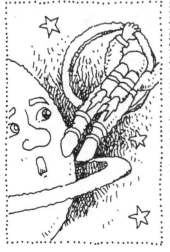   

Read the story.

Paul's Pasta

Paul wanted to make pasta salad. First, he put cooked pasta in a bowl. Second, he put yogurt in the bowl. Next, he added celery. Then, he added tomatoes. Last, he stirred.

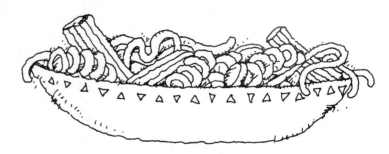

1. Why did the author write this story?

   _____

2. Read the sentences. Number them in the correct order.

   _____ He added celery.

   _____ He stirred.

   _____ He put cooked pasta in a bowl.

   _____ He added tomatoes.

   _____ He put yogurt in the bowl.

3. Write a sentence about a time you made or cooked something.

   _____

   _____

   _____

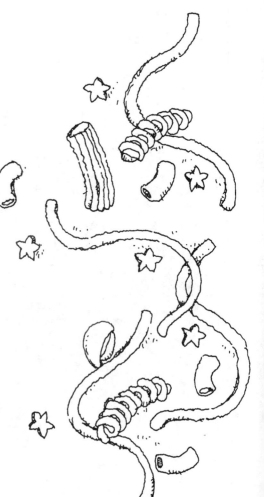

© Carson-Dellosa • CD-104840

Read the story.

Names

My name is Megan Lewis. Everyone has a name. My brother's first name is James. His middle name is William. His last name is Lewis. Our pets have names, too. My cat is named Fluffy and my fish is named Goldie. Even towns have names! The name of our town is Smithville. We used to live in Portland.

My name is Megan Lewis.

1. Use the words from the word bank to complete the chart.

| Portland | Fluffy | James | Smithville | Goldie | Megan |

People Names	Pet Names	Town Names

© Carson-Dellosa • CD-104840

Read the story.

School

A school is a place where people go to learn. At school, students learn how to read. They learn how to spell new words. They learn math. They study science. Some schools also have lessons in art and music. A school can help you learn about many new things.

Draw a line to match each book to its subject.

1.   A. Science

2.   B. Math

3.   C. Reading

4.   D. Spelling

5. What is your favorite subject in school?_____

6. What is the name of your school? _____

7. Why did the author write this story?

_____

_____

© Carson-Dellosa • CD-104840

Read the story.

All of the Animals

There are many kinds of animals. Three kinds of animals are mammals, birds, and reptiles.

Mammals have fur or hair. Baby mammals drink milk from their mothers' bodies. A whale is a mammal.

Birds are the only animals that have feathers. A robin is a bird.

Reptiles have scaly skin. Most reptiles lay eggs on the ground. An alligator is a reptile.

Read each sentence. Is the animal described a mammal, a bird, or a reptile? Write **M** for mammal. Write **B** for bird. Write **R** for reptile.

1. _____ Maggie brushes her hair.

2. _____ The turtle lays its eggs in the sand.

3. _____ The blue jay has lost a feather.

4. _____ The piglets drink their mother's milk.

5. _____ A gull has white feathers.

6. _____ The cat is cleaning its fur.

7. Why did the author write this story?

_____

_____

_____

Read the story.

Reduce, Reuse, Recycle

"I have a great idea," said Dante. "What if we put all the garbage in the world in a submarine. We could send it to the bottom of the ocean."

"That would cost too much money," said Maria. "And it would pollute the ocean. Pretty soon, the garbage would be floating in the water."

"How about sending all of the garbage to space?" Dante asked.

"That would pollute space! And it would cost too much money. I think we can help here on Earth," Maria added. "In my family, we recycle. We put plastic in one bin. We put paper in another bin. Glass and cans go in their own bins. Then, our garbage is remade into new products."

© Carson-Dellosa • CD-104840

Name_____

1. Help Dante and Maria recycle. Cut out the pictures. Glue them in the correct bins.

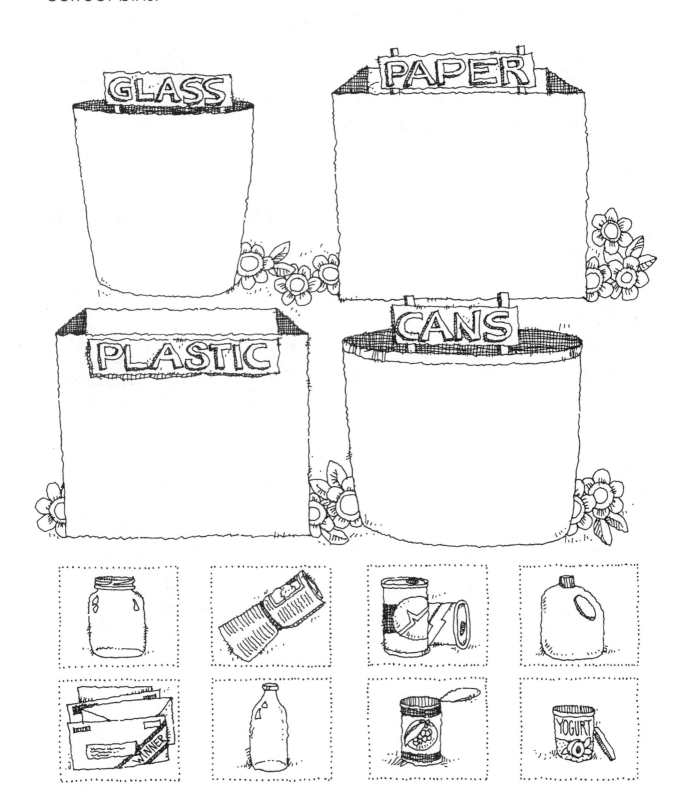

Read the story.

Months of the Year

There are twelve months in every year. March, April, and May are spring months. This is when flowers start to grow. June, July, and August are summer months. The weather is hot. It is fun to go to the beach. The fall months are September, October, and November. In some places, the leaves turn colors and the weather is cooler. December, January, and February are winter months. It is cold in these months.

1. Look at each picture. Label the picture **spring**, **summer**, **fall**, or **winter**.

   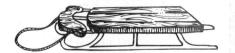

_____   _____   _____   _____

2. Write a sentence about something you can do in the summer but not in the winter.

_____

_____

3. Why did the author write this story?

_____

_____

_____

© Carson-Dellosa • CD-104840

Read the story.

Way Out West

Jill spends her summers on her dad's ranch. Jill rides horses. She helps take care of the horses, too. She wears jeans, boots, and a cowboy hat. Jill loves the horses and cows. She loves the ranch.

Circle the correct answer.

1. This story is mainly about
   _____.

   A. Jill's summers on a ranch

   B. Jill's riding lessons

   C. Jill's school year

   D. Jill's jeans and boots

3. Choose the words that tell about the main idea.

   A. jeans and boots

   B. horses and cows

   C. Jill and Dad

   D. ranch and summer

2. Another good title for this story is _____.

   A. "Jill's Horses"

   B. "Cows and Calves"

   C. "On the Ranch"

   D. "Summer"

4. Circle the hat that Jill might wear on the ranch.

© Carson-Dellosa • CD-104840

Read the story.

Money

Money has been used for many years to pay for things. Most people are paid money for their jobs. They use the money to buy food, clothes, and other things they need. There are two kinds of money: paper money and coins. Before there was money, people would **trade** one thing for another. A farmer would trade eggs for cloth, or a horse for land. Money gives us an easy way to buy what we need.

Circle the correct answer.

1. The main idea of this story is

   _____.

   A. how people pay for the things they need.

   B. how people get land for horses.

   C. how people work for money.

3. Which one of these is a **trade**?

   A. playing with toy cars

   B. giving a toy car for a bear

   C. having a car race

2. What did people do before there was money?

   A. They made their own money.

   B. They traded one thing for another.

   C. They went to the bank.

4. Which of these is a job?

   A. playing a game

   B. eating dinner

   C. teaching a class

© Carson-Dellosa • CD-104840

Name_____

Read the story.

Snakes

There are many kinds of snakes. Some snakes are big and long. Some snakes are small. Snakes are **cold-blooded**. This means they need the sun or heat to stay warm. Snakes do not have legs. They crawl on the ground. Snakes cannot run, but they can move very quickly.

Write **T** for true or **F** for false.

1. _____ The main idea of this story is to give facts about snakes.

2. _____ Another good title for this story would be "All About Snakes."

3. _____ Snakes cannot move.

4. _____ All snakes are the same size.

5. _____ This story tells how to take care of snakes.

6. What does **cold-blooded** mean?

_____

_____

7. Describe a snake you have seen.

_____

_____

Read the story.

Hobbies

A hobby is something special that a person likes to do. Some people like to collect things as a hobby. They will buy or trade stamps, coins, or comic books. Some people enjoy sports as a hobby. They like to play baseball, tennis, or soccer. Some people build things as a hobby. People build model airplanes, chairs, or even houses. Other kinds of hobbies are reading, playing music, and raising pets. What is your hobby?

Write a word in the blank to complete each sentence.

1. The main idea of this story is to tell about _____.

2. Some people build _____as a hobby.

3. Buying or trading _____is another kind of hobby.

4. A hobby is something special that a person _____ to do.

5. Which hobby from the story would you like the best? _____

6. Name a hobby you have or want to have. _____

© Carson-Dellosa • CD-104840

Read the story.

Up in the Sky, Down on the Ground

What do you think of when you think of a bird? Do you think of an animal spreading its wings? Do you think of it flying through the sky? Would you be surprised to find out that some birds cannot fly at all?

Kiwi birds cannot fly. Their wings are very tiny and will not hold them up. Ostriches cannot fly. Like kiwis, their wings are not strong enough to help them fly. Penguins cannot fly. Their small wings are more like swimming flippers. Their wings help them swim.

Circle the correct answer.

1. This story is mostly about _____.

    A. kiwis   B. ostriches   C. birds that cannot fly

2. The kiwi's wings are _____ .

    A. big   B. small   C. strong

3. A penguin's wings are _____ .

    A. big   B. like flippers   C. strong

4. Why did the author write this story?

    _____

    _____

    _____

Read the story.

Birds

There are many kinds of birds. The bluebird is blue and orange. It can lay up to six eggs. The robin has a red breast. It lays three or four eggs. The cowbird is black and brown. The bald eagle is a large bird. It lays from one to four eggs. The hummingbird is a very small bird. Sometimes it has a red spot on its throat.

Draw a line to match each bird to a detail that tells something about it.

1.	bluebird	A.	lays three or four eggs
2.	bald eagle	B.	blue and orange
3.	cowbird	C.	large bird
4.	hummingbird	D.	black and brown
5.	robin	E.	very small bird

6. Why did the author write this story?

_____

_____

© Carson-Dellosa • CD-104840

Name_____

Read the story.

Stars

Do you see the stars at night? They shine in the sky. They look like tiny points of light. But stars are not small. Some stars are as large as our sun. Some stars are even bigger than our sun. Here on Earth, the stars look very small to us. That is because they are so far away.

Circle the correct answer.

1. Some stars are _____.

   A. tiny points of light

   B. as large as our sun

   C. close to Earth

   D. very dark

2. Stars look small to us because _____.

   A. they are small

   B. they are so far away

   C. they shine so much

   D. they are suns

Write **T** for true or **F** for false.

3. _____ Stars look like tiny points of light.

4. _____ There are some stars that are bigger than our sun.

5. _____ You can see stars at night.

6. _____ Stars are close to us.

Read the story.

Starfish

Starfish live in the sea. But a starfish is not really a fish at all. It is an animal. It has tough, hard skin. This skin is covered with sharp bumps called spines. A starfish has five arms that make it look like a star. If one of these arms breaks off, the starfish can grow a new one. The mouth of the starfish is on the underside of its body.

Draw a line to match each part of the starfish to a detail that tells about it.

1. skin

A. can grow new ones

2. arms

B. on the underside of its body

3. mouth

C. sharp bumps

4. spines

D. tough and hard

5. Why did the author write this story?

_____

_____

_____

_____

© Carson-Dellosa • CD-104840

Name_____

Read the story.

At the Mall

Liza and her family are going to the mall. Dad wants to buy a new fan. Mom wants a vase for her flowers. John saved his money to buy a new toy truck. Liza wants a red scarf. After they go shopping, the family will go out to dinner.

1. Write the correct name under each picture.

What They Want to Buy

_____   _____

_____   _____

2. Where will the family go after shopping? _____

© Carson-Dellosa • CD-104840

Read the story.

Mt. Rushmore

    Mt. Rushmore is a mountain in South Dakota. It is carved with the faces of four presidents. One of the faces is that of George Washington, our first president. The other presidents on Mt. Rushmore are Thomas Jefferson, Abraham Lincoln, and Theodore Roosevelt. The carvings help us remember four great presidents.

Answer the questions.

1. How many presidents are carved on the mountain? _____

2. Who was our first president? _____

3. Where is Mt. Rushmore? _____

4. Why did the author write this story?

_____

_____

_____

© Carson-Dellosa • CD-104840

Read the story.

Moon Walk

What is it like to walk on the moon? Astronauts Neil Armstrong and Buzz Aldrin walked on the moon. They took pictures. People on Earth saw the pictures on television. The astronauts gathered rocks and dirt on the moon. Then they came back to Earth in *Apollo 11*. *Apollo 11* splashed into the ocean. The astronauts were heroes.

Circle **Yes** or **No** for each sentence.

1. Neil Armstrong watched television on the moon.   Yes   No

2. Buzz Aldrin walked on the moon.   Yes   No

3. The astronauts gathered rocks on the moon.   Yes   No

4. People took pictures of them on the moon.   Yes   No

5. *Apollo 11* splashed into the ocean.   Yes   No

6. Draw a picture of yourself walking on the moon.

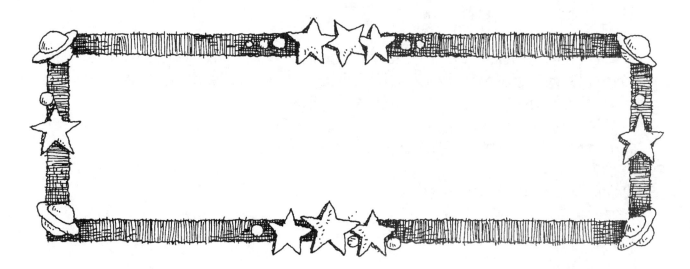

Read the story.

A Horse of a Different Color

"I cannot wait for our turn," said Noreen.

"I know," replied Fred. "It has been a long time since we rode horses."

"Is it time yet?" asked Kwan.

"Yes," said Anna. She turned to Will. "Are you ready?"

"I am not sure," said Will.

At the stable door, Will could not believe what he saw. All the horses had turned bright colors. "I do not feel so scared anymore," he said. He dashed to the blue horse.

"I want the green horse," cried Noreen.

"Red for Fred," said Fred.

Anna ran to the orange horse.

"The purple one is mine," said Kwan.

© Carson-Dellosa • CD-104840

1. Use details from the story to color each horse the correct color.

2. Where is the setting of this story? _____

Read the story.

The Earth Is a Puzzle

Have you ever thought of the earth's surface as a puzzle? The outer shell of the earth is called the crust. The crust is made up of plates—not the kind you put your food on. These plates come together like the pieces of a puzzle. Mountains can spring up when plates smash together. Earthquakes can occur when plates slide past each other.

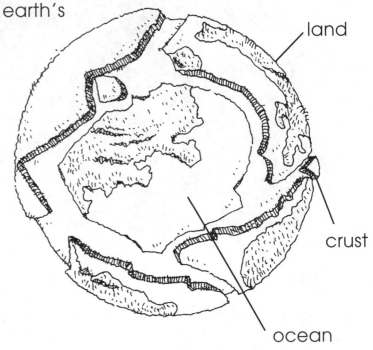

land

crust

ocean

Answer the questions.

1. What is the outer shell of the earth called? _____

2. How do earthquakes occur? _____

    _____

3. In your own words, tell about how the earth is like a puzzle.

    _____

    _____

    _____

    _____

© Carson-Dellosa • CD-104840

4. Cut out the puzzle pieces below. Glue them inside the circle to make a model of Earth.

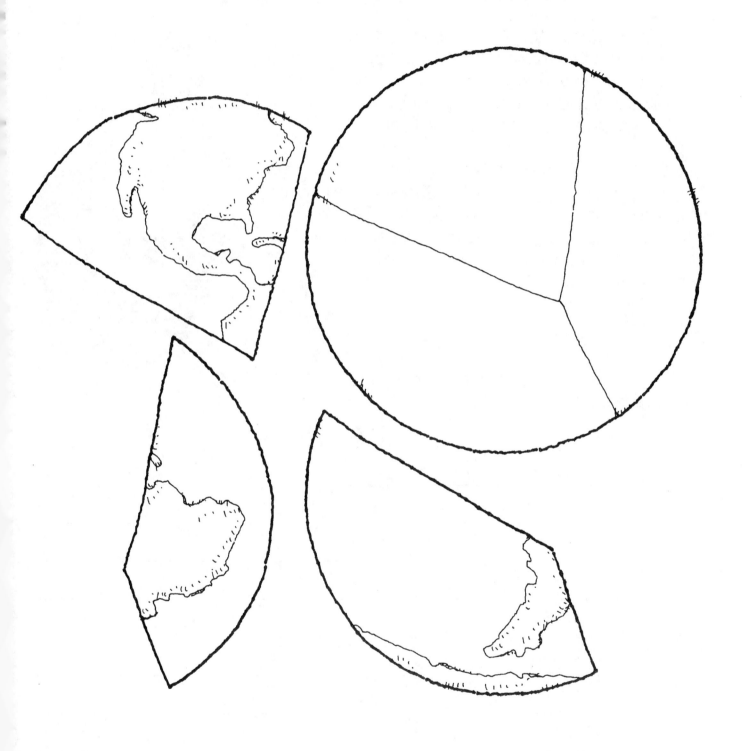

Read the story.

Talk to the Animals

Can a gorilla talk? Gorillas do not form words the way humans do. But they can make known what they want to say. One gorilla, Koko, learned sign language. She talked with her hands. And she understood words humans said.

Dr. Penny Patterson is the scientist who taught sign language to Koko. She showed Koko a picture of the two of them together. Penny pointed to Koko in the picture and asked, "Who is that?" Koko answered by signing her own name, Koko.

1. In your own words, write about what happened in the story.

_____

_____

_____

_____

_____

_____

_____

_____

© Carson-Dellosa • CD-104840

Read the story.

Weather

Weather is what it is like outside. Weather is always changing. One day it may be hot. The next day, it may get cool. Sometimes, it rains or snows. At other times, it may be foggy. Weather changes help us. When snow melts, it helps the ground get ready for new plants. Plants need both sun and rain to grow. Trees need cold weather to shed their leaves. Then, they can grow new ones.

Circle the correct answer.

1. Choose the sentence that tells about the whole story.

   A. Weather is always changing, and those changes help us.

   B. Weather is foggy in the spring.

   C. Weather needs to be cold for trees to grow.

2. Weather is _____.

   A. foggy and hot all the time

   B. what it is like outside

   C. what makes rain

   D. always the same

Use a word from the story to complete each sentence.

3. Rain, snow, and fog are all kinds of _____.

4. _____ need both sun and rain to grow.

5. Trees need _____ weather to shed their leaves.

Read the poem.

A Rabbit Poem

The rabbit is small and fast,
With a short and fluffy tail.
He has long ears that let him hear
Scary animals without fail.
Rabbits love to eat and eat!
They love the green, green grass.
They love to munch on vegetables
In a farmer's garden patch.

Answer each question. Be sure to write a complete sentence.

1. Write a sentence that tells about the whole poem.

    _____

    _____

    _____

2. Write a sentence to tell what rabbits look like.

    _____

    _____

    _____

3. Write a sentence to tell what rabbits like to eat.

    _____

    _____

    _____

© Carson-Dellosa • CD-104840

Read the story.

Football

Football is a fun game to watch or play. Players wear special uniforms. They wear pads to protect their bodies. They wear helmets to protect their heads. A football game is played with two teams. Each team tries to make a touchdown. Some players are good runners. Others can throw the ball well. It takes the whole team to win a football game.

Answer each question. Be sure to write a complete sentence.

1. Write a sentence that tells about the whole story.

    _____

    _____

    _____

2. Describe how to play of game of football.

    _____

    _____

    _____

3. What does it take to win a football game?

    _____

    _____

    _____

© Carson-Dellosa • CD-104840

Read the story.

Nelly Bly

Nelly Bly wanted to work for a newspaper. But in 1885, many people thought that women could not do this job. She did not give up. Finally she met a man who could give her a job. She proved to him that she could write good stories for his newspaper. She got the job! Nelly became well known as a **reporter**, someone who writes for a newspaper.

Circle the correct answer.

1. Which sentence tells about the whole story?

   A. Nelly Bly was a good writer.

   B. Nelly Bly did not give up, and she got her dream job.

   C. Nelly Bly did not think that women could write for newspapers.

3. What is a **reporter**?

   A. someone who teaches writing

   B. someone who writes for a newspaper

   C. someone who counts money for a bank

2. Why was it hard for Nelly to get a job as a reporter?

   A. Many people thought that women could not do this job.

   B. Many women worked for newspapers.

   C. Many people were out of work.

4. Would you want to be a reporter for a newspaper? Why or why not?

   _____

   _____

   _____

   _____

© Carson-Dellosa • CD-104840

Read the story.

Big Dogs, Little Dogs

If you are getting a dog, you need to choose between a big dog and a little dog. Both dogs can make great pets. Both dogs can be good friends. But there are differences between big dogs and little dogs.

A little dog can sit on your lap. It can live indoors and does not take up much space. Sometimes, a little dog can be noisy. Small dogs need to be trained not to bark too much.

A big dog may have to live outside. It will need more food and more space. Big dogs can guard your house. They can help you stay safe.

1. Use the Venn diagram to summarize details about cats and dogs.

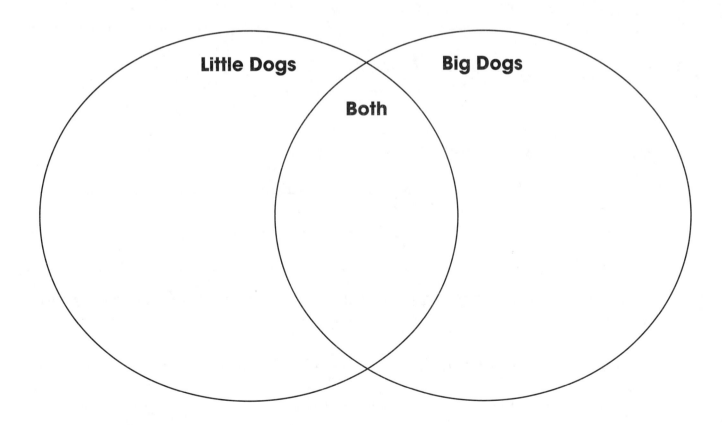

Little Dogs

Big Dogs

Both

© Carson-Dellosa • CD-104840

Read the story.

Snow

    Snow is small, white flakes of frozen water. Snow falls to the ground when the air is cold. If the ground is warm, the snow **melts**, or turns back into water. If the ground is cold, snow stays on the ground.

    When a lot of snowflakes fall quickly, it is called a **snowstorm**. When a snowstorm is a blizzard, the wind blows hard. During a **blizzard**, snow can end up in big piles called **snowdrifts**.

Write **T** for true or **F** for false.

1. _____ Snow is small flakes of frozen water.

2. _____ When snow melts, it freezes.

3. _____ When a lot of snow falls, it is called a snowdrift.

4. _____ A snowstorm is called a blizzard when the wind blows hard.

5. _____ Snow melts if the ground is warm.

6. _____ When snow falls quickly, it is called melting.

7. Why did the author write this story?

_____

_____

_____

8. Write a sentence about a time you or someone you know played in the snow.

_____

_____

© Carson-Dellosa • CD-104840

Name_____

Read the story.

Foxes

A fox looks a little like a dog. It has a pointed **snout** (or nose), big ears, and a bushy tail. Foxes often live in **burrows**, or holes in the ground. They hunt at night. They use their senses, such as sight, smell, and hearing, to help them hunt. Foxes eat **rodents** such as mice and squirrels. They also eat birds and frogs. Foxes are **clever**, or smart. This helps them live in the wild.

Circle the correct answer.

1. What is a **snout**?

    A. ears

    B. tail

    C. nose

    D. paws

2. What does **clever** mean?

    A. wild

    B. smart

    C. fast

    D. hunter

3. Which one of these is a **rodent**?

    A. a frog

    B. a bird

    C. a cat

    D. a mouse

4. What is a **burrow**?

    A. a hole in the ground

    B. a kind of nose

    C. a tree branch

    D. a kind of animal

5. Why did the author write this story?

    _____

    _____

Read the story.

The Days Grow Short

Justin watched a busy little mammal climb up the tree. Then it raced down again, looking for nuts. Justin knew that it was **hoarding** nuts, storing them for winter. The animal came back with an **acorn** in its mouth. "It found another nut!" thought Justin. "That little guy will be **prepared** when winter comes."

Circle the correct answer.

1. What is the mammal that Justin is watching?

   A. a squirrel

   B. a cat

   C. a mouse

   D. a dog

3. What is an **acorn**?

   A. a mammal

   B. a kind of nut

   C. a kind of tree

   D. a season

2. What does **hoarding** mean?

   A. eating

   B. racing

   C. storing

   D. climbing

4. What does **prepared** mean?

   A. warm

   B. hungry

   C. fast

   D. ready

5. Why did the author write this story?

   _____

   _____

© Carson-Dellosa • CD-104840

Read the story.

The Rodeo

A rodeo is a show for cowboys and cowgirls. One event is the bucking horse contest, where riders try to stay on wild horses for as long as they can. Another contest is barrel racing. In this contest, a cowgirl tries to quickly ride her horse around a set of barrels. There is also bareback riding, where a horse is ridden without a saddle. Prizes are given for each event.

Draw a line to match each word to its meaning.

1. rodeo

    A. riding a horse around barrels

2. bucking horse contest

    B. riding without a saddle

3. bareback riding

    C. riding a wild horse

4. barrel racing

    D. a show for cowboys and cowgirls

5. Why did the author write this story?

_____

_____

© Carson-Dellosa • CD-104840

Read the story.

Time

There are many ways that we measure time. A year is made of 365 days. A week has 7 days. One day is made up of 24 hours. Each hour is 60 minutes. One minute is made up of 60 seconds. How short is one second? You can blink your eyes one time in one second.

Circle the correct answer.

1. Which is the longest?

    A. a week

    B. an hour

    C. a minute

    D. a second

2. Which is the shortest?

    A. a year

    B. a day

    C. a week

    D. a minute

3. How many days are in a week?

    A. 7 days

    B. 5 days

    C. 6 days

    D. 8 days

4. Which is the shortest?

    A. 365 days

    B. 365 minutes

    C. 365 seconds

    D. 365 years

5. Why did the author write this story?

    _____

    _____

© Carson-Dellosa • CD-104840

Name_____

Read the poem.

Penguins and Robins

Who loves the cold? Penguins, that's who!
They dive and they swim right under the ice.
Robins go south when the warm weather stops,
And they don't fly back north until it is nice.
Penguins can't fly, but robins can soar.
They fly up to the clouds and back to their nest.
The black-and-white penguin waddles on snow,
And if it gets tired, it can slide for a rest!

Circle the correct answer.

1. Who loves the cold weather?

    A. penguins

    B. robins

2. Which birds fly?

    A. penguins

    B. robins

3. Which birds can swim?

    A. penguins

    B. robins

4. Who flies south when it gets cold?

    A. penguins

    B. robins

5. Why did the author write this poem?

    _____

    _____

Name_____

Read the story.

On the Coast

Los Angeles and New York are alike because they are both cities. Many movies and television shows are filmed in both cities. Los Angeles is on the West Coast. New York is on the East Coast. The weather stays warm in Los Angeles during the winter. The weather gets very cold in New York during the winter. Both cities can be fun to visit.

Use the Venn diagram to compare and contrast New York City and Los Angeles.

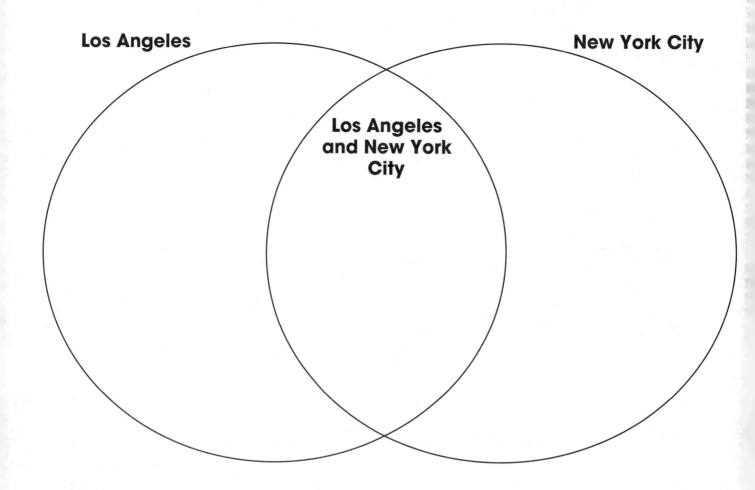

Los Angeles

New York City

Los Angeles and New York City

© Carson-Dellosa • CD-104840

Read the story.

Elephants and Giraffes

Elephants and giraffes are alike because they are mammals. They are different in many other ways. One animal has a long trunk and the other has a long neck. Both animals look for food, but they eat differently. The elephant uses its long trunk to pick up food and put the food in its mouth. The giraffe can eat leaves from tall trees because of its long neck and legs.

Write **T** for true and **F** for false.

1. _____ The elephant is a mammal, but the giraffe is not.

2. _____ The giraffe uses its long neck to reach for leaves in trees.

3. _____ The elephant has a long trunk and a long neck.

4. _____ The giraffe has a long neck and long legs.

5. _____ The elephant uses its trunk to put food in its mouth.

6. _____ The elephant looks for food, but the giraffe does not.

7. Why did the author write this story?

_____

_____

Read the story.

Queen for a Day

"The play is tomorrow. Are you ready?" Danielle asked Holly.

"I'm ready. I'm glad we get to practice while we wear our costumes," said Holly.

Danielle put on her crown. The colorful stones shone brightly. They matched her long, red queen's robe.

Holly put on her crown. She tugged at her purple queen's robe. "I think this robe is too small," she said.

"My robe fits just right," said Danielle.

"Queens, come to the stage with your costumes on," said Mr. Johnson.

Danielle and Holly dashed to the stage together.

© Carson-Dellosa • CD-104840

Name_____

How are Danielle and Holly alike and different? Circle **Yes** or **No** to answer each question.

1. Danielle and Holly are both queens in the play.   Yes   No

2. Danielle and Holly both wear crowns.   Yes   No

3. Danielle and Holly wear robes of different colors.   Yes   No

4. Danielle's robe and Holly's robe fit the same.   Yes   No

5. Draw a picture to show Danielle and Holly on the stage.

6. Write a sentence to describe a costume you have worn before.

_____

_____

© Carson-Dellosa • CD-104840

Read the story.

Farm or Beach?

"Let's plan our trip!" said Laura. "I want to go to see Aunt Kelly. She lives at the beach!"

"I want to go to see Grandma," said Sam. "Grandma lives on the farm!"

"Both are fun trips," said Laura. "Let's go to the beach! We can swim in the ocean."

"Let's go to the farm!" said Sam. "We can milk the cows!"

"Let's go to the beach!" said Laura. "We can build sand castles. We can catch crabs."

"Let's go to the farm!" said Sam. "We can see the baby chicks. We can feed the pigs."

"Let's go to the beach!" said Laura. "We can ride on a boat. We can go fishing. We can collect shells."

"Let's go to the farm!" said Sam. "We can ride on the tractor. We can dig up potatoes. We can get the eggs."

"We can do both!" said Laura. "Let's go to the beach to see Aunt Kelly. Then we'll take Aunt Kelly to see Grandma. We can do it all. And we can do it together!"

© Carson-Dellosa • CD-104840

1. How are a trip to the farm and a trip to the beach alike?

   _____

   _____

2. How are a trip to the farm and a trip to the beach different?

   _____

   _____

3. Cut out the pictures. On another sheet of paper, draw a beach and farm scene. Glue the pictures in the correct scenes.

Name_____

Amy, Pam, Miguel, and Clay all live in the same neighborhood. Look at the map and find their houses.

Map Facts

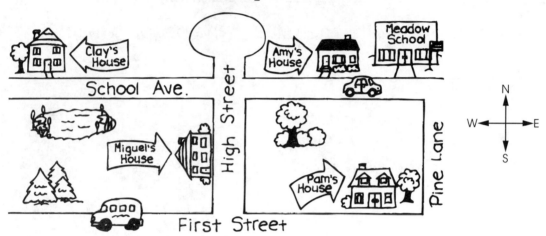

Circle the correct answer.

1. Which girl lives closer to the school?

   A. Amy

   B. Pam

2. Whose house does not sit on a street that goes left to right?

   A. Miguel's

   B. Pam's

3. Whose house has the most windows?

   A. Amy's

   B. Miguel's

4. Who lives across the street from a pond?

   A. Amy

   B. Clay

5. Who lives farther north?

   A. Clay

   B. Miguel

6. Who lives farther south?

   A. Amy

   B. Pam

© Carson-Dellosa • CD-104840

Read the letter.

Recycling

Dear Angela,

    In my family, we recycle. That means we put our trash into three bins. Plastic goes into one bin. Glass and cans go into another bin. Paper goes into the last bin. When the trash is taken away, it can be made into new things. I think this is the best way to take care of trash. If we put trash into the ground or into the sea, it will hurt the earth.

                         Your pen pal,

                         Maria

Circle the correct answer.

1. To recycle, Maria's family _____.

    A. puts trash into the ground

    B. puts trash into three bins

    C. puts trash into the sea

2. Recycled trash _____.

    A. is made into new things

    B. is thrown away

    C. is put in one big bin

3. If we put trash into the ground or the sea _____.

    A. it will make the earth better

    B. it will make paper

    C. it will hurt the earth

4. Fill in the chart.

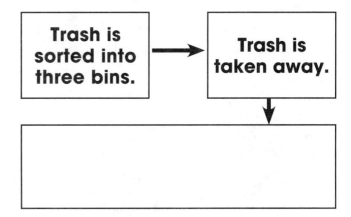

Read the story.

Animal Teamwork

Animals can work in teams. Some small fish eat food from the teeth of big fish. Then the big fish have clean teeth! Ants can get food from some small bugs. Then the ants keep the small bugs safe from other bugs. There are other animals that keep each other safe. One animal eats while the other animal keeps watch. They take turns eating. Animal teams can work well together.

Draw a line to match each cause to the effect.

1. A small fish eats food from the teeth of big fish.

2. Ants get food from small bugs.

3. Animals take turns keeping watch.

A. They take turns eating and stay safe.

B. Small bugs are kept safe by ants.

C. The big fish has clean teeth.

4. When have you been part of a team?

_____

_____

© Carson-Dellosa • CD-104840

Read the story.

Who Is First?

On Monday, Ms. Perez said, "The tallest student will be first in line."

On Tuesday, Ms. Perez said, "The shortest student will be first in line."

On Wednesday, Ms. Perez said, "The student wearing a dress will be first in line."

On Thursday, Ms. Perez said, "The student wearing a shirt with a number will be first in line."

On Friday, Ms. Perez said, "The student wearing his shirt tucked in will be first in line."

Ms. Perez's words caused a different student to be first in line each day. Write the correct day on which each student was first.

1.

_____

4.

_____

2.

_____

5.

3.

_____

_____

Read the story.

Deserts

A desert is very dry land. This land gets little rain. The air is hot during the day. At night, the desert becomes cool because the air cannot hold the heat from the day. The wind blows the sand into small hills called sand dunes. Some deserts have dirt instead of sand. Only a few kinds of plants and animals can live in such a hot, dry place.

Use words from the story to complete each sentence.

1. There are sand dunes in the desert because _____

_____.

2. A desert is a very dry land because _____

_____.

3. Only a few kinds of plants and animals can live in the desert because

_____.

4. The air in the desert becomes cool at night because _____

_____.

© Carson-Dellosa • CD-104840

Read the story.

Time for a Picnic

Mr. Walsh's class is planning a picnic. Everyone is going to bring something to eat or drink.

"I will get lemons and make something cold to drink," said Ava.

"I will get vegetables to make something crunchy to eat," said Carla.

"I will bring a cold and sweet dessert," said Anna.

"I will bring something sweet that my mom will bake," said Sam.

Draw a line to match what each student will bring to the picnic.

1. Carla

A.

2. Anna

B.

3. Sam

C.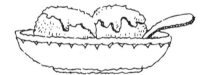

4. Ava

D.

5. Who is Mr. Walsh?

_____

Read each story. Circle the correct answer.

What Will They Do?

Justin wants to be an actor more than anything. He takes acting classes. He has been in plays. He has a chance to be in another play. He has to try out this afternoon. The phone rings. Justin's friend is calling. He wants Justin to come over this afternoon.

1.   What will Justin do?

   A. Justin will go to his friend's house.

   B. Justin will go to try out for the play.

Denise has been racing on her bicycle after school for two years. She is tired of bicycle races. She wants to try something new. Denise's teacher asks Denise to swim on the swim team after school.

2.   What will Denise do?

   A. Denise will swim.

   B. Denise will race on her bicycle.

© Carson-Dellosa • CD-104840

All animals have to eat to stay alive. Squirrels eat nuts. Whales eat sea plants and animals. Other animals eat many different things. A squirrel is hungry. It sees sea plants and nuts.

3. What will the squirrel do?

   A. The squirrel will eat the nuts.

   B. The squirrel will eat the sea plants.

Lucy loves her uncle. He is very special to her. Lucy wants to buy a birthday present for her uncle. He likes fishing, and she wants to buy him a fishing book. But she does not have enough money. Lucy saves her money for two months. Finally, she has enough money for the book.

4. What will Lucy do?

   A. Lucy will buy herself a new video game.

   B. Lucy will buy a fishing book for her uncle.

Read each story. Circle the correct answer.

What Would You Expect?

Isabel threw a little rock into a pond. Circles rippled out in the water around the little rock. More and more circles rippled until the ripples reached the shore.

1. What will happen if Isabel throws another little rock into the pond?

    A. All the water in the pond will spill out.

    B. Circles will ripple out into the water.

Ty never ate anything sweet. He went to Ginny's party. Ginny served sandwiches, popcorn, ice cream, and birthday cake. Ty had fun.

2. What did Ty eat?

    A. cake and popcorn

    B. sandwiches and popcorn

© Carson-Dellosa • CD-104840

The rain went on for hours and hours. Puddles formed in the streets. But the sun finally came out. The temperature rose to more than 100 degrees. The temperature stayed that hot for two days. There was no more rain.

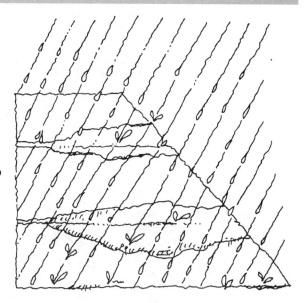

3. What happened after those two days?

   A. The puddles were gone.

   B. The puddles were bigger.

Erica loves to count. She counts everything. She counts leaves. She even counts clouds. The math test is tomorrow. Erica practices counting and adding all evening.

4. How will Erica do on the test?

   A. Erica will do well on the test.

   B. Erica will not take the test.

Read each story. Color the picture that shows what happens next.

And Then What Happens?

1. Judd loves to visit his grandmother. She lives next door. Judd finishes his homework early. And then what happens?

2. Ana starts to water the flowers. Her friend asks her to come over. They play. And then what happens?

© Carson-Dellosa • CD-104840

3. Pedro picks strawberries. He washes them well. He puts them in a bowl with pieces of banana. And then what happens?

4. Crystal is kind and helpful. She thinks of others and what they need. Crystal's brother comes home from school crying. And then what happens?

Read the story.

Happy Birthday

Jenna helped plan her brother's birthday party. She helped to shop for the party. She set the table. Here is a picture of the table right before the party.

Circle the correct answer.

1. What do you think the guests will be wearing?

   A. snow boots

   B. party hats

   C. mittens

   D. masks

2. What is one snack the guests will be eating?

   A. pasta

   B. soft drinks

   C. cake

   D. turkey

3. How old do you think Jenna's brother will be?

   A. two

   B. four

   C. five

   D. seven

4. What is one thing that Jenna bought for the party?

   A. a drum

   B. a grill

   C. teddy bears

   D. a tablecloth

© Carson-Dellosa • CD-104840

Read the story.

No More Trash!

Polly Packrat lived in the Green Woods. She liked to collect junk. She had rocks and cans. She had string, nuts, leaves, and sticks. She piled them all on her floor.

Mother Packrat looked at the mess. She said, "No more trash! Clean up this room!"

Polly filled up her wagon. She walked to the dump. She was sad. Then she saw a blue stone on the ground. It had rolled off the wagon. The pretty stone cheered Polly up.

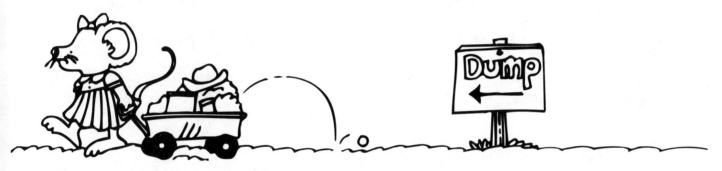

Write **T** for true or **F** for false.

1. _____ Real packrats can talk.

2. _____ Real animals have wagons.

3. _____ Polly Packrat is not like a real animal.

4. _____ Polly and her mother are characters in a story.

5. What does Polly like to collect? _____

6. Why was Polly sad? _____

_____

Read the story.

Clowns

Clowns are fun to watch. They are actors who like to make you laugh. Clowns wear makeup and wigs to look funny. They wear funny costumes and big shoes. Sometimes a clown will have a big, red rubber nose over his real nose. Clowns learn how to do tricks. You can see clowns in parades and at the circus.

Circle the correct answer.

1. Which sentence is true?

   A. Clowns are not real people.

   B. You can see clowns every day in your neighborhood.

   C. Clowns are actors dressed in special clothes and make-up.

   D. Clowns are real people who are strange.

2. Which things do clowns not wear?

   A. red rubber noses

   B. big shoes

   C. funny costumes

   D. police uniforms

3. Why do clowns do tricks?

   A. to cheat people

   B. to make people laugh

   C. to make people cry

   D. to learn things

4. Write one place you have seen a clown.

   _____

5. Why did the author write this story?

   _____

   _____

   _____

© Carson-Dellosa • CD-104840

Read the story.

Walking to Mars

Michelle learned all about the stars and planets. She read about the planet Mars. Mars was her favorite planet. Michelle wanted to see Mars herself. She pulled stars from the sky. She made stairs from the stars. Then, Michelle walked up the starry staircase to Mars.

Circle the correct answer.

1. In the story, how did Michelle go to Mars?

   A. She flew to Mars in an airplane.

   B. She went to Mars in a rocket.

   C. She built stairs to Mars and walked.

   D. She sailed to Mars in a boat.

2. How did Michelle build a staircase?

   A. out of stars

   B. out of clouds

   C. out of planets

   D. out of moons

3. Which helped you know that this story is not about a real event?

   A. Michelle learned about the stars.

   B. Michelle pulled stars from the sky.

   C. Michelle read about the planet Mars.

   D. Michelle's favorite planet was Mars.

4. What is your favorite planet? Why?

   _____

   _____

   _____

   _____

Read each story. Decide whether each could really happen. Circle the correct answer.

Could This Really Happen?

1. Zoe hurried. She did not want to be late for the baseball game. All of a sudden, wings grew on her back. She flew all the way to the field.

    A. This could really happen.

    B. This could not really happen.

2. The hot summer sun dried out the garden. Alex wanted his flowers to grow. He got the hose and watered his flowers.

    A. This could really happen.

    B. This could not really happen.

© Carson-Dellosa • CD-104840

3. David saved money all month. He wanted to buy a special gift
    for his grandfather. He bought a book about painting. He knew his
    grandfather would love it.

    A. This could really happen.

    B. This could not really happen.

4. Larry Lion found two mice that were balancing on a branch in the
    river. He helped the mice to the shore. Later, he found a baby zebra
    that was lost from his mother. The baby zebra asked Larry to help her.
    Larry was kind and helped the little zebra find his mother.

    A. This could really happen.

    B. This could not really happen.

Name_____

Read the letter.

The Moon

Dear Chang,

    Do you ever look at the moon at night? We learned about the moon at school today. It travels around Earth. It gets its light from the sun. Astronauts have gone to the moon in a spaceship. They have walked on the moon. They even brought back moon rocks to study. Would you like to walk on the moon some day? I would!

Your friend,

Evan

Circle **Yes** or **No** to answer each question.

1. Have astronauts really walked on the moon?

   Yes   No

3. Can you drive a car to the moon?

   Yes   No

2. Did astronauts fly to the moon in a spaceship?

   Yes   No

4. Does this picture show a real walk on the moon?

   Yes   No

5. Explain how you knew the answer to question 4. _____

_____

© Carson-Dellosa • CD-104840

Read the story.

Horseback Riding

Have you ever been horseback riding? Many people ride today because they think it is fun. People like to train horses to race or to jump. Long ago, horses were not kept as pets. People had to ride horses to go from one place to another. They also rode horses to hunt for food. Horses pulled wagons and helped to plow fields.

Write **F** for fact or **O** for opinion.

1. _____ Horseback riding is the best sport.

2. _____ Long ago, people needed horses to hunt for food.

3. _____ Horses are very pretty.

4. _____ Today, people like to train horses to race or jump.

5. _____ Horses are the smartest animals on Earth.

6. _____ Horses can pull wagons and plow fields.

7. Why did the author write this story?

_____

_____

© Carson-Dellosa • CD-104840

Read the letter.

Police

Dear Ashley,

    Today, a police officer came to our class. I thought she was the best speaker we have ever had! She talked about her job. She said that the police help keep people safe. They make sure people obey laws. Some police officers ride in cars. Others ride bikes. Some ride motorcycles. Some police even fly helicopters! I think that would be a great job. Don't you?

Yours truly,

Maggie

1. Circle the fact.

    A. Police officers are great speakers in class.

    B. Some police officers ride in cars.

    C. Flying a police helicopter would be a great job.

2. Circle the opinion.

    A. The police help keep people safe.

    B. Some police fly in helicopters.

    C. Flying a police helicopter would be a great job.

3. Would you like to be a police officer? Why or why not?

_____

_____

_____

_____

© Carson-Dellosa • CD-104840

Read the story.

Pilots

A pilot is a person who flies an airplane. Pilots go to special schools to learn how to fly planes. Some pilots fly planes for fun. Other pilots fly planes as their job. Pilots have to learn how to fly in all kinds of weather. They have to work with people on the ground to land planes safely. Being a pilot is an important job.

Draw a line to match the two parts of the sentences together.

1. Pilots go to special schools   A. for fun.

2. Some pilots fly planes   B. of weather.

3. Pilots have to fly in all kinds   C. flies an airplane.

4. A pilot is a person who   D. to learn how to fly planes.

5. Circle the fact.

   A. Pilots must have a lot of fun flying planes.

   B. It must be scary to fly in a storm.

   C. Some pilots fly planes as their job.

   D. All pilots are very brave.

6. Why did the author write this story?

_____

© Carson-Dellosa • CD-104840

Read the story.

Figs

Fig is the name of a fruit. It is also the name of a plant. The fruit grows on this plant. The plant can look like a bush or a tree. Fig plants grow where it is warm all year long. Many people like to eat figs. They can be eaten in cookies or fig bars. They can be canned. Sometimes figs are dried. You can also eat fresh figs.

Color the fig red if the sentence is a fact. Color the fig blue if the sentence is an opinion.

 1. Fig trees are pretty.

 4. Fig cookies are the best cookies.

 2. Fig plants grow where it is warm all year long.

 5. Fig is the name of both a fruit and a plant.

 3. Figs can be eaten in many ways.

 6. Figs taste best if you eat them fresh.

7. What does a fig plant look like?

_____

8. Where do fig plants grow?

_____

© Carson-Dellosa • CD-104840

Read the story.

The Storm

We looked out the window. A tornado was headed right to our house! We ran into the bathroom and closed the door. All three of us got into the bathtub. I could hear a loud roar. I thought it sounded like a train. I was scared. But, my baby brother thought it was fun to hide in the bathtub.

Later, I found out that summer is the time when most tornadoes happen. These storms can knock down houses and other buildings. Sometimes, the tornado can pick up a car or a tree right off the ground. We were lucky because our house was not hurt. We were not hurt, either!

Draw a line to match the two parts of the sentences together.

1. Tornados often happen   A. houses and other buildings.

2. A tornado can knock down   B. like a train.

3. A tornado makes a loud roar   C. in the summer.

4. A tornado can pick up   D. cars or trees.

5. Underline one fact in the story.

6. Circle one opinion in the story.

Read the story.

Agree to Disagree

Tia had a dog. Dion had a cat. Dion thought cats were prettier than dogs. Tia thought dogs made better pets than cats. Tia and Dion talked about the noises their pets made. Cats meow. Dogs bark. Dion said dogs were louder than cats.

Dion thought his cat was the best pet in the world. Tia thought her dog was the best pet in the world. Tia and Dion agreed to disagree.

Circle **F** if the sentence is a fact. Circle **O** if the sentence is an opinion.

1. Dion thought cats were prettier than dogs.   F   O

2. Tia thought dogs made better pets than cats.   F   O

3. Cats meow.   F   O

4. Dogs bark.   F   O

5. Dogs are louder than cats.   F   O

6. Tia thought her dog was the best pet in the world.   F   O

7. Do you think cats or dogs make better pets? Explain.

_____

_____

_____

_____

© Carson-Dellosa • CD-104840

Name_____

Read the story.

Eating Right

Some foods are good for you. They help your body grow. They help your teeth and bones become strong and healthy. Fruits and vegetables are good foods for you. Milk and things made with milk are good for you, too. Whole-grain crackers and bread make good and healthy snacks.

Some foods do not give your body the important things it needs to grow. Foods made with a lot of sugar, such as candy and cookies, are not as good for you. These foods are not good for your teeth. Foods with a lot of salt and fat are not good for your body.

Read each sentence. Write **T** for true or **F** for false.

1. _____ Potato chips are a healthy snack choice.

2. _____ Milk is better for your body than soda.

3. _____ Healthy food keeps your bones and teeth strong.

4. _____ Peanuts are a good after-school snack.

5. Why are cookies and candy not a healthy food choice?

_____

_____

Read the story.

The Stagecoach

People have not always had cars. Long ago, a stagecoach was the best way to go from one town to another. This big coach needed four or six horses to pull it. The stagecoach carried people. It also took mail from one place to another. Stagecoach trips could take days. The ride was bumpy and hard. But it was better than other ways of travel.

Circle the correct answer.

1. Why did people use stagecoaches?

    A. because they liked horses

    B. because they liked bumpy trips

    C. because there were no cars

2. Why do you think riding in a stagecoach was bumpy and hard?

    A. because the roads were not good

    B. because the wheels were the wrong size

    C. because the horses moved too fast

3. What is one reason that a stagecoach would be better than riding a horse?

    A. It would protect you from rain or snow.

    B. Riding a horse would be slower.

    C. You could not ride a horse on bumpy roads.

4. What did the stagecoach not do?

    A. take mail from place to another

    B. carry people to other towns

    C. use an engine

© Carson-Dellosa • CD-104840

Name_____

Read the story.

Astronauts

An astronaut is a person who travels in space. Only a few people can become astronauts. After a person is picked, he or she has to go to a special school. Astronauts can spend years learning everything they need to know for space travel. They must know all about their spaceships. They must be smart. They must be very healthy. Astronauts work hard to get ready for their jobs.

Circle the correct answer.

1. Why does an astronaut have to go to a special school?

   A. because space travel is not taught in other schools

   B. because traveling in space is fun

   C. because astronauts must be healthy

2. Why do you think that an astronaut needs to be smart?

   A. to learn about the stars

   B. to help out if something goes wrong

   C. to be able to exercise

3. Which of these people do you think would make the best astronaut?

   A. a gardener

   B. a skater

   C. a scientist

4. How long can it take an astronaut to learn everything he needs to know?

   A. weeks

   B. years

   C. days

Read the story.

I Can!

Sandra stamped her little leg. "I can't do anything right!" she buzzed. She watched her honeycomb crumble. Sandra sat down in the soft honey and put her head in her hands.

Just then, Sandra heard her friend Rusty bark. He was hurt. Sandra zoomed down and saw a thorn stuck in Rusty's paw. At first, she was afraid to help her friend. "I won't do it right," she buzzed. Her little heart raced.

But then Sandra had a plan. She put honey on a leaf. She stuck the leaf to the thorn. She pulled it out! Rusty wagged his tail.

Circle the correct answer.

1. Sandra is a _____ ? dog   bird   bee

2. Sandra's friend is a _____ ? bee   dog   bird

3. Sandra is _____ ? mean   kind   rude

4. At the end of the story, the friend is _____ ? sad   scared happy

5. Draw a picture of Sandra and her friend.

© Carson-Dellosa • CD-104840

Name_____

Read the story.

Glassfish

Glassfish are small fish. Most live in the ocean, but some live in freshwater in India. You can see through a glassfish's skin. You can even see its bones! Some people have glassfish for pets. They are hard to raise in a tank. They live better in the sea.

Circle the correct answer.

1. How do you think the glassfish got its name?

   A. because it is full of water

   B. because it is made from glass

   C. because you can see through its skin

2. Which one is a glassfish?

   A.

   B.

   C.

3. Why do you think glassfish live better in the sea?

   A. because they are made of glass

   B. because they want to live in tanks

   C. because the sea is their natural habitat

4. What kind of fish is a glassfish?

   A. large

   B. small and clear

   C. dark-colored

© Carson-Dellosa • CD-104840

Read each story. Then, circle the picture that shows what each family will take to a picnic.

Yum! Yum!

1. Kwan gathers lemons. His uncle cuts them. Kwan squeezes the juice into a pitcher. He adds sugar and water. Kwan puts in lemon slices and ice. He stirs. Kwan and his uncle are making:

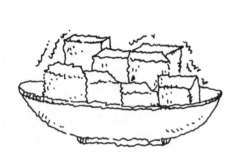 

2. Whitney and her dad put flour, sugar, water, and an egg into a bowl. Whitney adds melted chocolate. They stir the mixture. Then she puts the mixture in a pan. Whitney's dad puts the pan in the oven. Frosting will come later. Whitney and her dad are making:

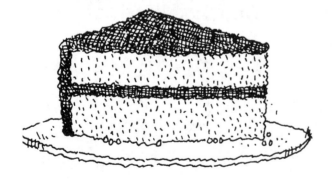 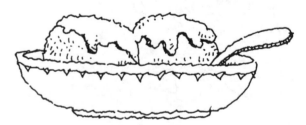

© Carson-Dellosa • CD-104840

3. Alvin and his mom buy a roll of dough at the grocery store. His mom cuts the dough into circles. Alvin puts them on a long metal sheet. His mom puts them in the oven. Alvin and his mom are making:

4. Cindy gets lettuce, tomatoes, and cucumbers from her garden. Her grandfather cuts them into pieces. Cindy puts the pieces into a bowl. Cindy and her grandfather are making:

5. Draw a picture of your favorite food to take to a picnic.

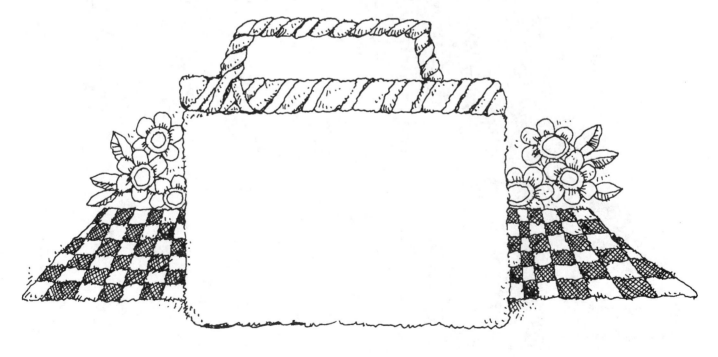

Read the story.

It's Cold Outside!

"We should go play outside," said Myra to her grandma.

"It sure is cold," said Grandma. "Do you have your mittens?"

"Yes," said Myra. She and Grandma stepped outside.

Myra and Grandma played in the tall white drifts. They made big white balls and threw them. Little flakes began to fall. "Looks like we will get a few more inches today," Myra said.

© Carson-Dellosa • CD-104840

What happened **before** Myra and her grandma went outside?
Circle **Yes** or **No** for each sentence.

1. The hot sun shone for many hours.   Yes   No

2. Myra played outside in her shorts.   Yes   No

3. Snow fell for many hours.   Yes   No

4. Myra swam outside in the swimming pool.   Yes   No

5. Why did Myra think they would get have more snow?

   _____

   _____

   _____

6. Draw a picture of Myra and her grandma playing outside.

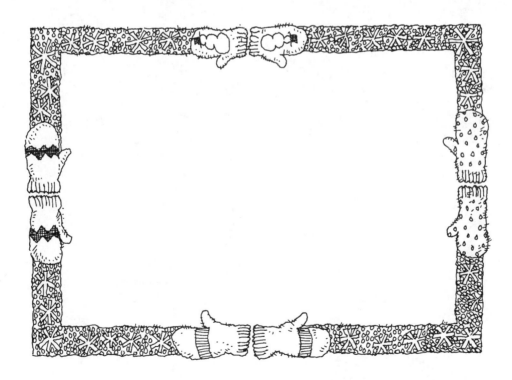

Read the poem.

Ouches in Our Pouches

What goes in our pouches?

Bees in our pouches?
No! Ouches in our pouches!

Ice skates in our pouches?
No! Ouches in our pouches!

Jacks in our pouches?
No! Ouches in our pouches!

Cactus in our pouches?
No! Ouches in our pouches!

Roses in our pouches?
No! Ouches in our pouches!

Porcupines in our pouches?
No! Ouches in our pouches!

We want softness in our pouches!
No more ouches in our pouches!

© Carson-Dellosa • CD-104840

1. Look at the squares. Write the correct words from the poem under each picture.

2. Cut out the square that shows what the kangaroo wants in her pouch. Glue the square to the kangaroo's pouch.

Read the story.

Eli Elephant

Eli Elephant loves to garden. He waters the plants with his trunk. He eats the vegetables as soon as they are ripe. Eli is gray. He has a long trunk. He wears a hat to keep safe from the hot sun. He loves to wear old, soft overalls.

Answer the questions.

1. What does Eli love to do? _____

2. What does he water the plants with?_____

3. What does Eli wear to keep safe from the sun? _____

4. What does Eli love to wear?_____

5. Is this story reality or fantasy? _____ How do you know?

    _____

© Carson-Dellosa • CD-104840

Name_____

Read the story.

Guiding the Way

Tara is not able to see. But she has a guide dog to help her. Her guide dog, Delia, helps in many ways. Delia guides Tara to school. Delia is very careful as she and Tara cross the street. Tara can tell Delia to go straight, to turn, or to stop. Delia listens carefully. Tara gives Delia big hugs. Delia snuggles with Tara and gives her big kisses.

1. Choose words from the word bank to complete the graphic organizer.

| angry | careful | helpful | kind | loving | mean | selfish |

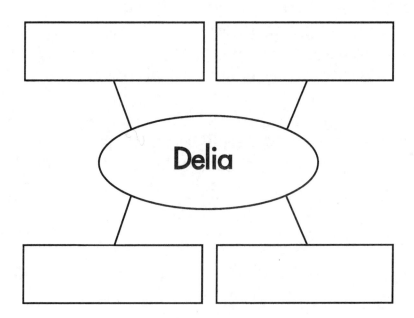

2. Why is a dog like Delia important to Tara?

_____

_____

© Carson-Dellosa • CD-104840

Read the story.

Wah Chang

Wah Chang loved to draw. He drew pictures of cowboys when he was only three! Wah studied hard to learn more about art. By the time Wah was eight, he was showing his art work in art shows. People read about him in the newspaper.

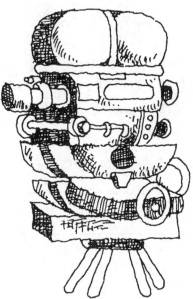

Something very sad happened when Wah was eleven. His mother passed away. Wah was so very sad. But he gathered his strength and went on.

Wah worked for Walt Disney Studios when he was still young. He worked on movies, such as *Pinocchio* and *Bambi*. Then Wah got very sick. He had polio. Some people who had polio died. Some were never able to walk again. But Wah worked long and hard. He was able to walk with special braces on his legs.

Wah continued to work on special effects. He worked for many films and television shows, such as *Star Trek*. Even though he had many hard times, Wah Chang always worked to bring joy to others.

© Carson-Dellosa • CD-104840

1. Circle words from the word bank that tell about Wah Chang.

kind	artist	lazy
hard worker	talented	worried
mean	never stopped trying	

2. In your own word bank, write words that tell about you. Then, use those words to write sentences about yourself.

Read the story.

Olivia's Job

Olivia is very smart. She loves to read. She likes to argue. She gives many good reasons when she argues.

Olivia likes to help people. Once, one of her friends bought a yo-yo at a store. The yo-yo broke the first time her friend tried to play with it. Olivia went to the store with her friend. Olivia talked to the manager. The manager took back the yo-yo and gave Olivia's friend a new one.

Olivia often thinks about what she would like to do when she gets older.

© Carson-Dellosa • CD-104840

Name_____

What jobs does Olivia think about? Unscramble the letters to find out. Write each job name.

1. Olivia thinks about being a _____ and helping sick people in a hospital.   cootdr

2. Olivia thinks about being a _____ and working with students in a classroom.   chetrae

3. Olivia thinks about being a _____ and going to court to talk to a judge.   lyrewa

4. Olivia thinks about being a _____ and helping sick animals.   tve

5. Which job do you think would be best for Olivia? Why?

    _____

    _____

    _____

    _____

6. Which job do you think you would like to have when you get older?

    _____

    _____

Read the story.

Bink! Bonk!

Bonk wanted to learn to skate. Bink had been skating for a long time. Bonk asked Bink for a skating lesson. Bonk had knee pads. Bink said, "I do not need those." Bonk had a helmet. Bink said, "I do not need that."

Bonk took one step and boink! Bonk fell. Bink laughed. "Might as well go home," Bink told Bonk.

"I will not give up," said Bonk. Bonk fell again. But finally, Bonk took one small step and did not fall.

"Just beginner's luck," said Bink. Bink skated backward.

"Be careful," cried Bonk. "Watch where you're going."

Bink tripped on a rock. She skinned her two knees. CLONK! CLONK! CLONK! CLONK!

"I will help you up," said Bonk. "Then, maybe I can help you with another thing or two."

© Carson-Dellosa • CD-104840

1. Choose words from the word bank to describe Bink and Bonk. Write the words in the circles around their names.

kind	careful	rude
careless	mean	does not give up

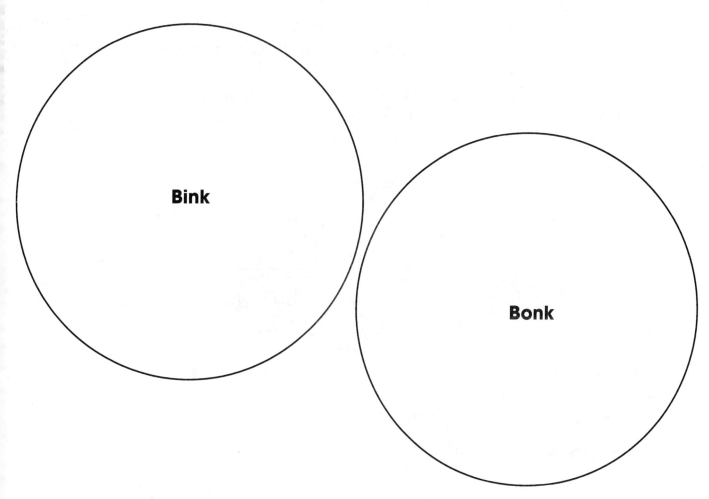

2. Write a sentence to describe each character.

_____

_____

_____

_____

Read the story.

The Taxi Ride

Jasper and his father got into the taxi at the airport. Jasper said, "Please take us to the Grand Hotel."

"Yes, sir!" said the taxi driver. "That is on Hudson Street."

Jasper watched as numbers clicked on a box next to the driver. "That is called a meter," said Jasper's father. "It tells how much we will pay the driver."

The taxi crossed a bridge. It went down one street and then turned right. After a while, the driver said, "Here we are." He drove Jasper and his father right to the door of the hotel. Jasper's father paid the driver when they got out.

Answer the questions.

1. Where did the taxi take Jasper and his father? _____

2. Where was the Grand Hotel? _____

3. What machine tells how much to pay the taxi driver? _____

4. What did the father do when he got out of the taxi?

_____

5. Is this story reality or fantasy? _____ How do you know?

_____

_____

_____

© Carson-Dellosa • CD-104840

Read the story.

Camping Trip

Maria and her mother went camping in the woods. First, they put up a tent under a big tree. Then, they built a fire. As it got dark, Maria and her mother cooked dinner over the fire. They ate marshmallows for dessert. It was warm by the fire. It was cozy in the tent. Maria heard the crickets chirping before she fell asleep.

Circle the correct answer.

1. Where did Maria and her mother camp?

   A. in a city

   B. by a stream

   C. in the woods

2. Where did Maria and her mother sleep?

   A. by the fire

   B. in a tent

   C. in the car

3. Where was it warm?

   A. in the car

   B. in the tent

   C. by the fire

4. What did Maria hear before she fell asleep?

   A. crickets

   B. frogs

   C. a storm

5. Write a sentence about a time you slept outside or at a friend's house.

_____

_____

_____

Every story happens at a place and time. Read each story. Cut out each square at the bottom of page 99. Glue it next to the story it matches.

Where and When?

1. The clock showed midnight. Two mice friends sat in their home. They talked about the things they wanted to do. One wanted to eat all the cheese in the world. The other wanted to break all the mice traps in the world.

2. Julio and Ethan went to school early in the morning. They sat at their desks. The teacher read a book about dolphins. Then, Julio and Ethan wrote books of their own.

© Carson-Dellosa • CD-104840

3. The year is 3010. Ryan and Yuri zoom into space. Their spaceship moves faster than the speed of light. They race toward the moon.

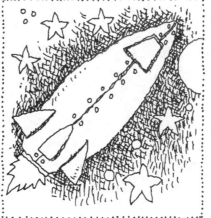

Read the story.

Icebergs

There are big sheets of ice on the South Pole and near the North Pole. Sometimes pieces break off from these sheets. The pieces float out in the ocean. They are called **icebergs**.

If you were crossing the ocean, you might see an iceberg. Icebergs can be big. Some are as big as mountains. But often, only a tip of the iceberg can be seen above the water. Most of the iceberg is below water. As icebergs float into warmer water, they melt and become part of the ocean's water.

Circle the correct answer.

1. If you were on an iceberg, it would be_____.

   A. cold and slippery

   B. warm and cozy

   C. dry and hot

2. Icebergs can be_____.

   A. as big as mountains

   B. too cold to melt

   C. as big as an ocean

3. Icebergs may be hard to see because _____.

   A. they are as big as mountains

   B. they are floating away

   C. only a tip shows above the water

4. What happens to an iceberg?

   A. It becomes part of the North Pole again.

   B. It turns into a mountain.

   C. It melts and becomes part of the ocean's water.

© Carson-Dellosa • CD-104840

Name_____

Read the story.

A Day Off

Grace's family does something special on Labor Day. They all go to a hospital in their town. Everyone in her family is given a job to do. Grace gets to bring books to the patients, the people in the hospital rooms. Because Grace's family works, some of the hospital workers can have the day off. After the family is done working, they have a picnic in the park.

Circle the correct answer.

1. Why does Grace's family go to the hospital on Labor Day?

   A. because they are hurt

   B. because they are ill

   C. because they are helping

2. What does Grace do on Labor Day?

   A. She takes books to patients.

   B. She watches fireworks.

   C. She cooks for the patients.

3. Why does Grace's family work at the hospital?

   A. They think it is fun.

   B. They let hospital workers have a day off.

   C. They like to take books to people.

4. What does Grace's family do at the end of the day?

   A. They go swimming.

   B. They go riding.

   C. They have a picnic.

Read the story.

At the Beach

Hector and his family went to the beach. Dad went swimming. Mom read a book.

Hector and his brother wanted to build a sand castle. They used pails to make part of the castle. They filled the pails with wet sand. Then they turned them upside down to make towers. They used shells to make the castle look nice.

At the end of the day, the tide came in. The waves washed over the castle. It turned back into sand on the beach.

Draw a line to match the two parts of the sentences together.

1. Hector and his family

2. Hector and his brother wanted to

3. The two brothers used pails

4. Hector and his brother used shells

5. At the end of the day, the waves

A. build a sand castle.

B. to make towers for the castle.

C. went to the beach.

D. washed over the castle.

E. to make the castle look nice.

© Carson-Dellosa • CD-104840

Name_____

Read the story.

A Fall Day

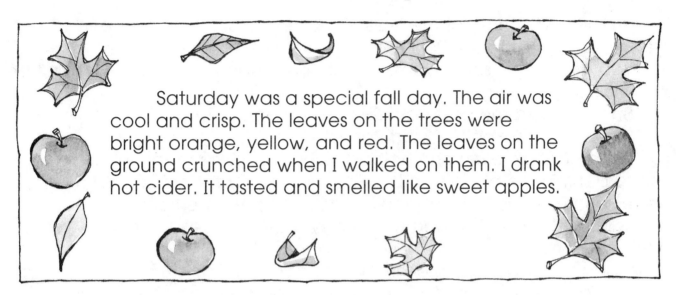

Saturday was a special fall day. The air was cool and crisp. The leaves on the trees were bright orange, yellow, and red. The leaves on the ground crunched when I walked on them. I drank hot cider. It tasted and smelled like sweet apples.

Use words from the story to complete the web.

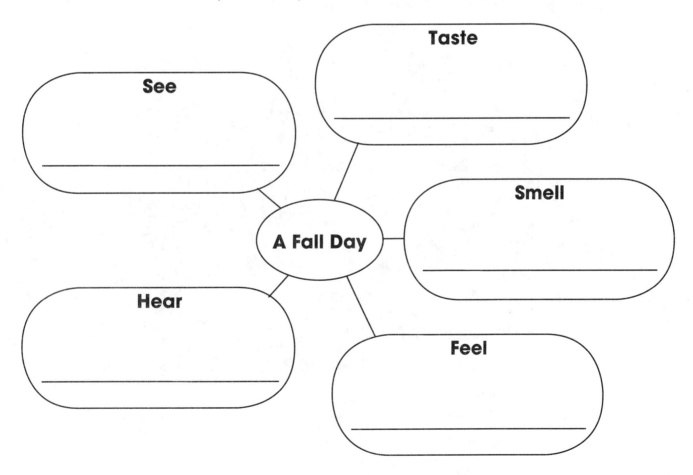

Read the story.

I Can Do It!

"We're going to enter the baking contest," said Ivy. "We need one more person on our team. Roberto, will you be on our team?"

"You know me," said Roberto. "I am not good at contests. I will not be able to do anything right."

"But you bake the best cake. Please be on our team."

"Maybe just this once," said Roberto.

At the contest, everyone helped. Everything was mixed in the bowl. "Time to put it in the pan," said Ivy. She turned around quickly. Bam! The bowl fell off the table. All of the mix oozed out onto the floor.

"What will we do?" asked Ivy. Her eyes grew wide. "Help, Roberto. You are the only one who can mix it right. Please help."

Roberto took a deep breath. His hands shook. "If you need me, I can do it," he said. Roberto mixed everything in the bowl. He moved fast!

After the contest, Roberto said to his friends, "I guess I can do things right. I am glad we were in the contest together."

© Carson-Dellosa • CD-104840

Name_____

1. Write about the story on page 104. Tell what happens in the beginning, middle, and end of the story.

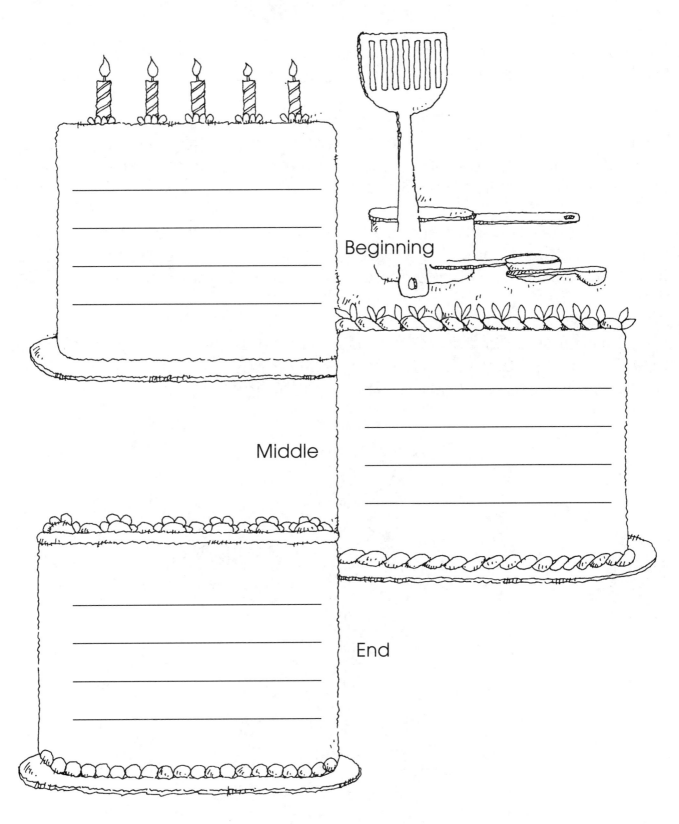

Beginning

Middle

End

© Carson-Dellosa • CD-104840

Read the story.

Family Help

"Help me!" yelled Papa Squirrel. "I cannot walk. I cannot run." Papa Squirrel laid on the ground. A cat tiptoed nearby.

"I will help!" yelled Brother Squirrel. He ran down the tree. Brother Squirrel tried to lift Papa. "Papa, you are too heavy for me," said Brother Squirrel. Brother Squirrel ran back up the tree. "Papa needs help!" cried Brother Squirrel to Grandma Squirrel.

Grandma and Brother raced down the tree. "We will help you!" they yelled. "Papa, you are still too heavy for us." Brother looked up to the top of the tree. "Come down," Brother called to Sister Squirrel. She zoomed down the tree.

Brother and Grandma and Sister Squirrel used their paws and noses to push Papa. "Papa, you are not too heavy for us," said Brother and Grandma and Sister Squirrel. They pushed Papa up the tree. All of the squirrels were safe.

© Carson-Dellosa • CD-104840

1. Write about the story on page 106. Tell what happens in the beginning, middle, and end of the story.

Beginning

_____
_____
_____
_____

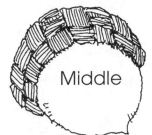

Middle

_____
_____
_____
_____

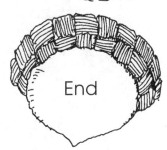

End

_____
_____
_____

2. Think of a story you would like to tell. Plan the beginning, middle, and end. Then, write the story on another sheet of paper.

Beginning: _____

_____

Middle: _____

_____

End: _____

_____

Read the story.

Who's Afraid?

"We are going to the beach for my birthday!" said Libby. "Can you come?"

"I do not know," said her friend Lynn. "I'm afraid of the water."

"Please come," said Libby. "You do not have to get in the water. Just come and have some birthday cake." Lynn agreed.

At the beach, Lynn played in the sand. She built sand castles. She threw beach balls. She wrote her name in the sand with a stick.

As Lynn picked up a beach ball, she heard a shout. "Help," yelled Libby. "I hurt my toe on a rock. I cannot walk back."

"The water scares me," cried Lynn.

"Please," yelled Libby. "I need you."

Lynn dashed toward Libby. She got to the edge of the water. Her heart raced. I do not know if I can do it, she thought. She looked at her friend. Libby needs me, she thought. Lynn walked bravely into the water. She helped Libby out of the water.

"Thank you," said Libby. "You are a true friend."

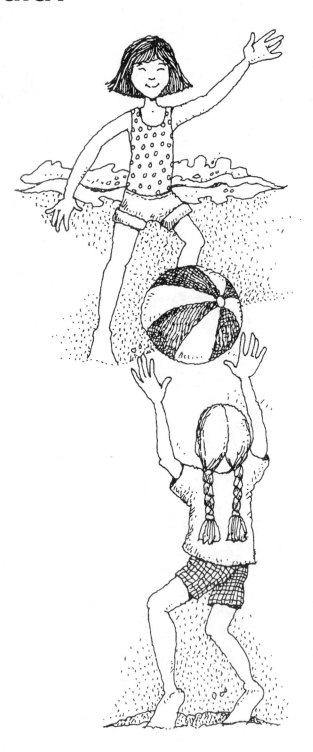

© Carson-Dellosa • CD-104840

1. Write about the story on page 108. Tell what happens in the beginning, middle, and end of the story.

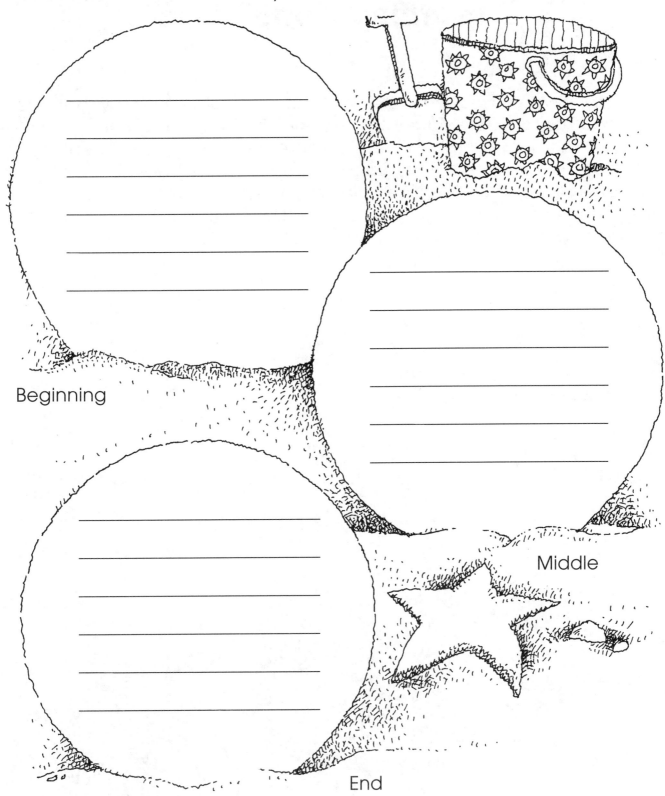

Beginning

Middle

End

Read the letter.

Learning About Bees

Dear Grandma,

    This week in school we learned about bees. Did you know that bees work together and help each other? In their home, called a **hive**, there are three kinds of bees. One kind are the worker bees. The worker bees all have jobs. They clean the hive. They take care of the baby bees. Some of them fan their wings to keep the hive cool! Worker bees are also the ones you see flying in the garden. They get nectar from the flowers. The nectar is turned into honey back at the hive.

                                    Love,

                                    Cory

Write words from the letter in the blanks to complete each sentence.

1. Worker bees clean the _____.

2. Worker bees take care of _____ bees.

3. Worker bees fan their _____ to keep the hive cool.

4. Worker bees get _____ from the flowers.

5. What is a **hive**? _____

© Carson-Dellosa • CD-104840

Name_____

Read the story.

Lunch Time

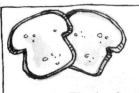

Justin was hungry. He wanted to eat lunch.
Here's what he did:
First, Justin got out two slices of bread.
Second, he opened a jar of peanut butter and a jar of jelly.
Then, Justin spread peanut butter on one piece of bread.
Next, he spread jelly on the other piece of bread.
Last, he put the two slices of bread together.

Circle the correct answer.

1. What did Justin do first?

    A. He spread peanut butter on bread.

    B. He got out two slices of bread.

    C. He spread jelly on bread.

2. What did Justin do after he had spread peanut butter and jelly on the bread?

    A. He opened a jar of jelly.

    B. He put the two slices of bread together.

    C. He ate the two slices of bread.

3. Why did Justin get out the bread, jelly, and peanut butter?

    A. Because he liked bread.

    B. Because he wanted to play.

    C. Because he was hungry.

4. What did Justin make?

    A. a sandwich

    B. a cookie

    C. a sundae

Read the story.

The Lost Pet

Yasmin got a hamster for her birthday. She named the hamster Squeak. On the day after her birthday, Yasmin looked in her pet's cage. Squeak was missing! Yasmin looked all around the room. She looked under the chairs. She looked under the table. Then, she heard a soft squeak. She ran to the cage. Squeak was there! He had been asleep under a pile of wood shavings.

Write **T** for true or **F** for false.

1. _____ The first place Yasmin looked was in Squeak's cage.

2. _____ Next, Yasmin looked under the table.

3. _____ Squeak was asleep under a pile of feathers.

4. _____ Yasmin ran upstairs to look for Squeak.

5. _____ It turned out that Squeak was not really lost.

6. _____ Squeak is a cat.

© Carson-Dellosa • CD-104840

Read the story.

Earthquake!

All earthquakes cause shaking. Some earthquakes cause problems. Most earthquakes in the United States happen near the Pacific Ocean. Many buildings there are built in a special way. This helps keep people safe during an earthquake. No earthquakes happen in outer space.

Use the words from the word bank to complete each sentence.

Some	All	Most	Many	No

1. _____ buildings near the Pacific Ocean are built in a special way.

2. _____ earthquakes cause shaking.

3. _____ earthquakes happen in outer space.

4. _____ earthquakes cause problems.

5. _____ earthquakes in the United States happen near the Pacific Ocean.

© Carson-Dellosa • CD-104840

Read the story.

Through the Hoop

Lillie and Maria play on a basketball team called the Tigers. The Tigers are playing the Bears. Each team gets two points for each basket. The score is 4 to 4. It's a tie so far. Lillie's heart pounds. She bounces the ball. She looks for a teammate. She passes the ball to Maria. Swoosh! Two points!

A member of the Bears team grabs the ball. She races to the other end of the court. She makes a basket.

Lillie jumps into action. She bounces the ball all the way back to her basket. She sinks the ball through the basket. One of the Bears scoops up the ball, runs across the court, and makes another basket. The game is over.

1. Make a scoreboard to show who wins. Write a 2 for every basket each team makes.

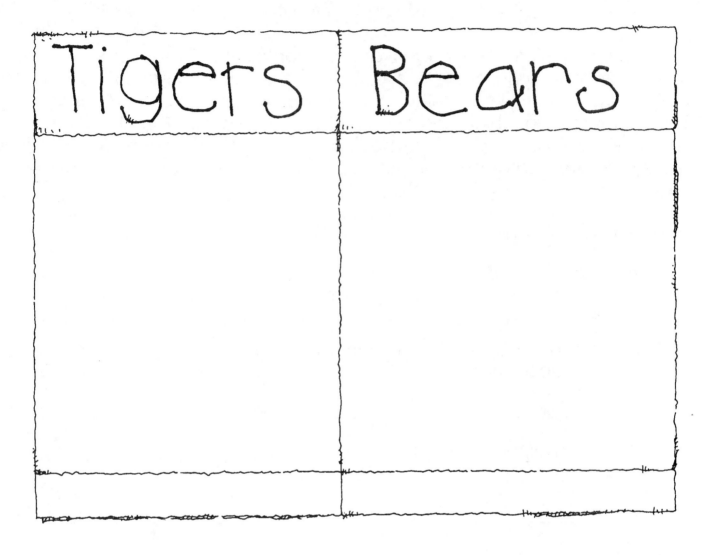

Tigers	Bears

2. Who won the game? _____

3. Where is the setting? _____

4. What do you think the two teams will do now? _____

_____

_____

© Carson-Dellosa • CD-104840

Read the story.

Hurricanes

Hurricanes form during the warmest months of the year. The sun heats the ocean, and water starts to evaporate. The warm, moist air rises, and cool air rushes to replace it. The moist air is pushed up where clouds form. The clouds start touching and swirling around in a circle. The circle forms a storm that can be hundreds of miles across. The center of the storm is called the **eye of the hurricane**. The eye has calm winds. In the center of the eye, blue sky can be seen.

Answer the questions.

1. In what months do you think most hurricanes form?

   _____

2. Why do the people that live in the mid-western United States not have to worry about hurricanes?

   _____

3. Do you think there are hurricanes at the North Pole? _____
   Why or why not?

   _____

   _____

4. What is the **eye of the hurricane**? _____

   _____

© Carson-Dellosa • CD-104840

Read the story.

Pet Match

Jackie has a job. She gives baths to her friends' pets. Her friends are coming to pick up the pets. Help Jackie match the pets to their owners.

Read the clues. Cut out the pets. Glue each pet below its owner's name.

Kenya's pet is a dog.

The cat belongs to the girl near flowers.

A pig is between the dog and the cat.

A hamster is between the dog and a horse.

1. Jeremy   2. Adrian   3. Kenya   4. Bob   5. Ashley

© Carson-Dellosa • CD-104840

Read the story.

The Good Doctor

When you do not feel well or have hurt yourself, you can tell your parents. If they cannot help you, they can take you to a doctor. The doctor will check you. She might ask you questions. The doctor will tell you what you need to do to get better. You might have to take medicine. You might have to stay home from school so you do not share your illness with others. You might have to rest or do special exercises. Soon, you will feel better.

When pet, farm, or zoo animals get sick or hurt, they cannot tell anyone. Animal owners must watch their pets to know when they are hurt or sick. When a pet is sick, the owner will take it to a special animal doctor. This is a veterinarian, or vet. If a large farm or zoo animal is ill, the veterinarian may visit it.

A veterinarian goes to school and studies how to help or treat sick and hurt animals. This is just like your doctor who went to school to learn how to help you.

Animals cannot tell the vet where it hurts or how it feels. The vet must examine the animal. Often the animal does not understand that the vet wants to help. The vet will ask the owner questions to help find out what is wrong. The vet will tell the owner what he needs to do to help the animal get better. They might have to take medicine. Sick animals might have to stay away from healthy animals so others do not get sick. They might have to rest or do special exercises. Soon the animal will feel better.

© Carson-Dellosa • CD-104840

Name_____

Think about what a veterinarian does and answer the questions.

1. How are a doctor and a veterinarian alike?

   _____

   _____

   _____

2. How are a doctor and a veterinarian different?

   _____

   _____

   _____

3. How is treating a sick person and a sick animal alike?

   _____

   _____

   _____

4. How might treating a baby be like treating an animal?

   _____

   _____

   _____

5. Would you want to be a veterinarian? Why or why not?

   _____

   _____

   _____

   _____

Read the story.

Unusual Fish

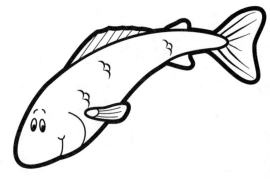

Cavefish are whitish in color. They grow to be about 5 inches (13 cm) long. They live in caves and underground rivers. Some have eyes, but they cannot see. Others have no eyes at all.

Flying hatchetfish are a shining silver color. They grow to be about 4 inches (10 cm) long. They swim near the top of the water. They jump out of the water and fly through the air to catch insects.

A walking catfish can live in and out of water. It can move from one lake to another by walking on land. It has no legs so it pushes itself along with its tail, using its strong fins to move the front of its body.

Make up a new kind of fish. Describe your fish. Then, draw a picture to match your description.

_____
name of your fish

_____
size

_____
color(s)

_____
where it lives

_____
characteristic

© Carson-Dellosa • CD-104840

Read the story.

Magpies

The magpie is a noisy bird. It likes to copy sounds other birds make. These birds can be tamed. They can even be trained to speak simple words.

The magpie cannot be trusted by other birds. It will often steal food right from their nests.

Magpies often build their nests in thorny bushes for protection. The nests are big with a dome-shaped top. A hole is left in one side for the magpies to get in and out of the nest. They lay five to ten greenish-blue eggs that have brown and tan spots. Magpies may live about 12 years.

Answer the questions.

1. If you were going to choose a bird for a pet, would you choose a

   magpie? Why or why not? _____

   _____

2. Do you think other birds should build their nests near a magpie's nest?

   Why or why not?_____

   _____

3. How do thorn bushes protect a magpie? _____

   _____

Read the story.

Building Up

Kayla's class is building a block city. They have colored blocks. The blocks are green, orange, and red. Group A is building a store. Group B is making a bank. Group C is building a library. Group D is working on a school.

Read the chart to answer the questions.

	Green blocks	Orange blocks	Red blocks
Group A	5	3	0
Group B	6	7	1
Group C	0	4	5
Group D	1	2	7

1. Which group is using the most red blocks?

   _____

2. Which group is using no red blocks?

   _____

3. Which group is using the fewest orange blocks?

   _____

4. Which group is using the most blocks altogether?

   _____

5. Which group is using the fewest blocks altogether?

   _____

© Carson-Dellosa • CD-104840

Answer Key

Page 5
1. 3, 1, 2; 2. C; 3. B

Page 6
1. 3, 4, 1, 2; 2. Answers will vary but may include that Jan will chase after Jay the jackrabbit.

Page 7
1. 3, 4, 2, 1; 2. under its eyes; 3. at night

Page 8
1. boy blowing out candles; 2. clown blowing up balloons; 3. clown holding balloon dog; 4. clown standing on head; 5. clown disappearing in smoke

Page 11
1. the planets; 2. One of his moons lost a ring. 3. (placed in correct order 1-4) Sally talking to smiling Pluto, Sally talking to sad-faced Mars, Sally jetting away from Saturn with ring, smiling Mars with ringed moon

Page 12
1. to explain how to make pasta salad; 2. 3, 5, 1, 4, 2; 3. Sentences will vary.

Page 13
1. People Names: Megan, James; Pet Names: Fluffy, Goldie; Town Names: Smithville, Portland

Page 14
1. B; 2. D; 3. A; 4. C; 5. Answers will vary. 6. Answers will vary. 7. to explain how a school helps students learn different things

Page 15
1. M; 2. R; 3. B; 4. M; 5. B; 6. M; 7. to give information about mammals, birds, and reptiles

Page 17
1. Glass: glass jar, glass bottle; Paper: newspaper, mail; Plastic: milk jug, yogurt container, Cans: soft drink cans, vegetable can

Page 18
1. spring, summer, fall, winter; 2. Sentences will vary. 3. to explain what months are in each season

Page 19
1. A; 2. C; 3. D; 4. Cowboy hat (far right) should be circled.

Page 20
1. A; 2. B; 3. B; 4. C

Page 21
1. T; 2. T; 3. F; 4. F; 5. F; 6. to need sun or heat to stay warm; 7. Answers will vary.

Page 22
1. hobbies; 2-3. Answers will vary. 4. likes; 5-6. Answers will vary.

Page 23
1. C; 2. B; 3. B; 4. to explain why some birds can fly and others cannot

Page 24
1. B; 2. C; 3. D; 4. E; 5. A; 6. to give information about different types of birds

Answer Key

Page 25
1. B; 2. B; 3. T; 4. T; 5. T; 6. F

Page 26
1. D; 2. A; 3. B; 4. C; 5. to describe a starfish

Page 27
1. fan: Dad, truck: John, scarf: Liza, vase: Mom; 2. out to dinner

Page 28
1. four; 2. George Washington; 3. South Dakota; 4. to give information about Mt. Rushmore

Page 29
1. No; 2. Yes; 3. Yes; 4. No; 5. Yes; 6. Drawings will vary.

Page 31
1. Will: blue horse, Noreen: green horse, Fred: red horse, Anna: orange horse, Kwan: purple horse; 2. a horse stable

Pages 32–33
1. the crust; 2. when the crust's plates slide past each other; 3. Answers will vary but should be in student's own words and should reflect important points in selection. 4. Earth "puzzle" should match Earth illustration.

Page 34
1. Answers will vary but should be in student's own words and include important details from the passage.

Page 35
1. A; 2. B; 3. weather; 4. Plants; 5. cold

Page 36
1. Answers will vary. Sentence should indicate that the poem tells what rabbits look like and what they like to eat. 2. Answers will vary. Sentence should indicate that rabbits are small, have fluffy tails, and have long ears. 3. Answers will vary. Sentence should indicate that rabbits like to eat green grass and vegetables.

Page 37
1. Answers will vary. Sentence should indicate that the story tells about the sport of football and how it is played. 2. Answers will vary. Sentence should indicate that the game is played with two teams. Each team tries to make a touchdown. 3. It takes the whole team to win a football game.

Page 38
1. B; 2. A; 3. B; 4. Answers will vary.

Page 39
1. Little Dogs: can sit on your lap, can be noisy, do not take up too much space, can live indoors; Big Dogs: may live outside, need more food and space, can guard a house, can help you stay safe; Both: are great pets, can be good friends

Page 40
1. T; 2. F; 3. F; 4. T; 5. T; 6. F; 7. to give information about snow and the different kinds of snowstorms; 8. Answers will vary.

Page 41
1. C; 2. B; 3. D; 4. A; 5. to describe foxes

© Carson-Dellosa • CD-104840

Answer Key

Page 42

1. A; 2. C; 3. B; 4. D; 5. to explain how a squirrel prepares for the winter by gathering nuts

Page 43

1. D; 2. C; 3. B; 4. A; 5. to give information about the events at a rodeo

Page 44

1. A; 2. D; 3. A; 4. C; 5. to give information about the different ways to measure time

Page 45

1. A; 2. B; 3. A; 4. B; 5. to compare and contrast penguins and robins

Page 46

Los Angeles: on West Coast; weather stays warm in winter, New York: on East Coast; weather gets very cold in winter, Both: cities, movies and television shows filmed in both, fun to visit

Page 47

1. F; 2. T; 3. F; 4. T; 5. T; 6. F; 7. to compare and contrast giraffes and elephants

Page 49

1. Yes; 2. Yes; 3. Yes; 4. No; 5. Drawings will vary but should show Danielle in a red robe that fits and Holly in a purple robe that is too small. 6. Answers will vary but should include details about the costume.

Page 51

1. Both would be fun trips; 2. Answers will vary but may include: On a farm, you could collect eggs, ride a tractor, dig up potatoes, feed pigs, watch chicks, or milk cows. At the beach, you could swim in the ocean, catch crabs, ride a boat, build a sand castle, fish, and collect shells. 3. Check students' drawings.

Page 52

1. A; 2. A; 3. B; 4. B; 5. A; 6. B

Page 53

1. B; 2. A; 3. C; 4. Trash is made into new things.

Page 54

1. C; 2. B; 3. A; 4. Answers will vary.

Page 55

1. Wednesday; 2. Tuesday; 3. Thursday; 4. Monday; 5. Friday

Page 56

1. the wind blows the sand into small hills; 2. the land gets little rain; 3. it is such a hot and dry place; 4. the air cannot hold the heat from the day

Page 57

1. B; 2. C; 3. D; 4. A; 5. the teacher

Pages 58–59

1. B; 2. A; 3. A; 4. B

Pages 60–61

1. B; 2. B; 3. A; 4. A

Answer Key

Pages 62–63
Pictures colored: 1. boy playing basketball with grandmother; 2. flowerpot of flowers with water overflowing; 3. boy and older man eating fruit salad; 4. girl comforting brother

Page 64
1. B; 2. C; 3. C; 4. D

Page 65
1. F; 2. F; 3. T; 4. T; 5. junk; 6. Polly did not want to get rid of her junk.

Page 66
1. C; 2. D 3. B; 4. Answers will vary. 5. to give information about clowns, their costumes, and the tricks they can do

Page 67
1. C; 2. A; 3. B; 4. Answers will vary.

Pages 68–69
1. B; 2. A; 3. A; 4. B

Page 70
1. Yes; 2. Yes; 3. No; 4. No; 5. Answers will vary but may include that the moon does not cry.

Page 71
1. O; 2. F; 3. O; 4. F; 5. O; 6. F; 7. to explain horseback riding of long ago and horseback riding today

Page 72
1. B; 2. C; 3. Answers will vary.

Page 73
1. D; 2. A; 3. B; 4. C; 5. C; 6. to give information about pilots

Page 74
1. blue; 2. red; 3. red; 4. blue; 5. red; 6. blue; 7. a bush or tree; 8. where it is warm all year

Page 75
1. C; 2. A; 3. B; 4. D; 5. Answers will vary but may include that tornados can pick up cars and trees. 6. Answers will vary but may include that the author thought the tornado sounded like a train.

Page 76
1. O; 2. O; 3. F; 4. F; 5. O; 6. O; 7. Answers will vary but should include an opinion.

Page 77
1. F; 2. T; 3. T; 4. T; 5. They contain large amounts of sugar and are not good for your teeth.

Page 78
1. C; 2. A; 3. A; 4. C

Page 79
1. A; 2. B; 3. C; 4. B

Page 80
1. bee; 2. dog; 3. kind; 4. happy; 5. Drawings should show a bee and a dog.

Page 81
1. C; 2. A; 3. C; 4. B

Pages 82–83
1. lemonade; 2. cake; 3. cookies; 4. vegetable salad; 5. Drawings will vary.

Page 85
1. No; 2. No; 3. Yes; 4. No; 5. Because it

© Carson-Dellosa • CD-104840

Answer Key

started to snow again. 6. Drawings will vary but should show a grandmother and girl throwing snowballs.

Page 87
I. bees, skates, jacks, soft, porcupine, cactus, roses; 2. The soft baby joey goes in the mother kangaroo's pouch.

Page 88
I. garden; 2. his trunk; 3. a hat; 4. soft overalls; 5. fantasy, Elephants do not wear clothes or garden.

Page 89
I. Delia: kind, helpful, loving, caring; 2. Answers will vary but should reflect understanding of the love and help the dog and human give to each other.

Page 91
I. hard worker, kind, talented, artist, never stopped trying; 2. Word banks and sentences will vary.

Page 93
I. doctor; 2. teacher; 3. lawyer; 4. vet; 5. Answers will vary but students will likely choose lawyer based on evidence from the selection. 6. Answers will vary.

Page 95
I. Bink: rude, careless, mean, Bonk: kind, careful, does not give up; 2. Sentences will vary but should show understanding of the characters.

Page 96
I. Grand Hotel; 2. Hudson Street;

3. meter; 4. paid the driver; 5. Reality, because people can take taxis to places in real life.

Page 97
I. C; 2. B; 3. C; 4. A; 5. Sentences will vary.

Pages 98-99
I. at midnight in a mouse home picture; 2. early morning picture; 3. spaceship picture

Page 100
I. A; 2. A; 3. C; 4. C

Page 101
I. C; 2. A; 3. B; 4. C

Page 102
I. C; 2. A; 3. B; 4. E; 5. D

Page 103
Answers will vary but may include: See: leaves, Taste: cider, Hear: leaves crunching, Feel: cool air, Smell: apples or cider

Page 105
I. Beginning: Ivy asks Roberto to enter a baking contest. Middle: The cake mix is ready, but spills. End: Roberto mixes the new cake and is happy he entered the contest.

Page 107
I. Beginning: Papa falls out of tree and a cat is nearby. Middle: Different squirrels try to help. End: Three squirrels work together to push Papa up the tree, and he is safe. 2. Stories will vary.

Answer Key

Page 109
1. Beginning: Libby invites Lynn to the beach. Middle: They play and then Libby gets hurt. End: Lynn walks into the water and helps Libby.

Page 110
1. hive; 2. baby; 3. wings; 4. nectar; 5. a home for bees

Page 111
1. B; 2. B; 3. C; 4. A

Page 112
1. T; 2. F; 3. F; 4. F; 5. T; 6. F

Page 113
1. Many; 2. All; 3. No; 4. Some; 5. Most

Page 115
1. Scoreboard should show a total of eight points for each team. 2. It was a tie. 3. a basketball court; 4. Answers will vary but may include play another game.

Page 116
1. Answers will vary but should include warm months such as May, June, July, August, and September. 2. Answers will vary but should include that the mid-western part of the United States is not near an ocean.
3. Answers will vary but should include that the North Pole is too cold for hurricanes to form. 4. the center of the storm

Page 117
1. horse; 2. hamster; 3. dog; 4. pig; 5. cat

Page 119
Answers will vary but may include: 1. Both go to school to learn how to help the sick and hurt, both ask questions, both help; 2. Doctors help people, vets help animals;
3. Both take medicine, both might have to rest or do special exercises, both might have to stay away from healthy people or animals;
4. Babies cannot tell doctors how they feel.
5. Answers will vary.

Page 120
Answers will vary.

Page 121
1. Answers will vary. 2. No, the magpie cannot be trusted and it might steal food.
3. The thorns protect the eggs from predators.

Page 122
1. Group D; 2. Group A; 3. Group D; 4. Group B; 5. Group A

© Carson-Dellosa • CD-104840